T0388522

GAMER CITIZENS

This book examines the politics of being a gamer in the digital age with an in-depth study of the communities of gamers who populate live-video streaming sites.

This text offers an innovative theoretical and methodological study of gamers in their community. It explores gamers as citizens and asks how gamers are political in view of their activities on stream. Ilya Brookwell examines how gamers live out their daily lives on live-video streams and how they use their associated new platforms and tools, including live-video streams such as Twitch.tv and online web fora, to engage with "live-video politics". It explores the relationship between gamers, gaming, and streaming, highlighting how gamers develop a notion of self that is fundamentally located in community. Gamers consequently create, inhabit, as well as inherit a political world. With streaming communities offering unique insights into what it means to live in a digital age, the book explores how gamers find hopeful openings, as well as limits, through streaming. The book highlights how gamers can take an active role in politics and democracy in a digital age.

Interesting reading for undergraduate students, postgraduate researchers, and academics of media, cultural and communication studies, video game studies, and digital media studies.

Ilya Brookwell is Assistant Professor of Media and Cultural Studies at the University of California, Riverside, USA. His research centers on video gamers, live-streaming, virtual reality (VR), and online community, particularly as these intersect with politics. His current research focuses on the emergent technologies of VR and asks how we find social immersion in a digital age. His series of published articles includes work on gamer citizens, emojis as civic duty, and the virtual reality community.

GAMER CITIZENS

Live-Video Politics in a Digital Age

Ilya Brookwell

NEW YORK AND LONDON

Designed cover image: Arsenii Palivoda/Getty Images

First published 2024
by Routledge
605 Third Avenue, New York, NY 10158

and by Routledge
4 Park Square, Milton Park, Abingdon, Oxon, OX14 4RN

Routledge is an imprint of the Taylor & Francis Group, an informa business

© 2024 Ilya Brookwell

The right of Ilya Brookwell to be identified as author of this work has been asserted in accordance with sections 77 and 78 of the Copyright, Designs and Patents Act 1988.

All rights reserved. No part of this book may be reprinted or reproduced or utilised in any form or by any electronic, mechanical, or other means, now known or hereafter invented, including photocopying and recording, or in any information storage or retrieval system, without permission in writing from the publishers.

Trademark notice: Product or corporate names may be trademarks or registered trademarks, and are used only for identification and explanation without intent to infringe.

Library of Congress Cataloging-in-Publication Data
Names: Brookwell, Ilya, 1984- author.
Title: Gamer citizens : live video politics in a digital age / Ilya Brookwell.
Description: New York, N.Y. : Routledge, 2024. | Includes bibliographical references and index.
Identifiers: LCCN 2023058520 (print) | LCCN 2023058521 (ebook) | ISBN 9781032371337 (paperback) | ISBN 9781032376219 (hardback) | ISBN 9781003341079 (ebook)
Subjects: LCSH: Video gamers--Political activity. | Video games--Political aspects. | Streaming video--
Classification: LCC GV1469.34.P65 B76 2024 (print) | LCC GV1469.34.P65 (ebook) | DDC 794.8/4--dc23/eng/20240131
LC record available at https://lccn.loc.gov/2023058520
LC ebook record available at https://lccn.loc.gov/2023058521

ISBN: 978-1-032-37621-9 (hbk)
ISBN: 978-1-032-37133-7 (pbk)
ISBN: 978-1-003-34107-9 (ebk)

DOI: 10.4324/9781003341079

Typeset in Sabon
by KnowledgeWorks Global Ltd.

CONTENTS

Preface	*vi*
Introduction	1
1 A Politics of Being Gamers	14
2 Encountering Gamer Citizens	44
3 Not a Game	64
4 Ludic Divides	86
Conclusion: Live Video Politics	117
Index	*134*

PREFACE

The first time I heard of live streaming a video game was in the autumn of 2011. I had just completed my Master's thesis in the field of theory and policy studies in education, and, having finalized my project about educational video games, I was ready to rekindle my personal interest in gaming and allocate more of my time and attention towards some of the newest upcoming titles. As a returning gamer, also acting upon a reversal of one of ethnography's central tasks, namely—to make the familiar strange and the strange familiar, I was hoping to make what was once familiar to me familiar again. I aimed to find joy in gaming and to reconnect with my old social networks. For many years, those networks had flourished on the official websites of game studios as well as on unofficial discussion fora such as Reddit and Kotaku, but most importantly, they had been centred on YouTube, a video platform that, by 2011, was well mature and a popular place for gamers to post their guides, playthroughs, exploits, as well as news and game reviews. When I asked a close friend of mine what games he was playing and whether I should consider joining him, his response took me by surprise: "Check out a few live streams", he explained. "I usually just watch gameplay these days instead of playing. Sometimes I see what looks fun and try it myself".

Somehow, watching live streams of video games seemed counterintuitive and not altogether appealing. After all, it was actually playing the games that made them special, or at least this was conceptually and fundamentally how I understood them to be different from older media such as movies or television programmes. How good were these streams anyway? Would I really get anything of worth out of watching someone play on a live-stream—anything that was any improvement over pre-recorded footage? I did not actually tune in to my first live-stream until much later, in May of 2012, while I was awaiting the release of a much-anticipated new game—notably one that was also on the wish lists for a vast number of my fellow gamers. I was unsatisfied once more with my access to relevant information and details for some of its features and content. The game (which I will leave unnamed) had been in development for more than ten years, yet leading up to its release, there simply did not appear to be enough coverage of it from any of my usual media channels. I kept searching until I came upon a channel on YouTube led by a particularly "hardcore" gamer and a self-proclaimed "no-lifer" who was offering precisely what I was looking for, namely all the information about all the strategies as well as insights and full guides on the game. In a video, he introduced himself as rebranded and reimagined—no longer a "YouTuber" but henceforth a "streamer". What is more, he was informing his followers and new viewers alike that now anyone could continue to watch his gameplay live, sixteen hours per day, streaming on Twitch.tv (Twitch).

Who was this streamer? Was he serious about broadcasting himself for such incredible lengths of time? What is more, what did it mean to be "hardcore" and to be a part of a team of "no-lifers"? It seemed clear to me that Twitch offered this streamer and his community—one that I was prospectively about to join—an opportunity for leadership and, quite contrary to their own claims, a pathway into a gamer life filled with meaning, passion, and drive. My initial quest to revisit games and gaming had led me to this gamer, an encounter ultimately leading to the core focus of this book.

I offer this story to exhibit how my own initial journey onto Twitch—the digital site which I chiefly examine—was marked by significant doubt and scepticism of the new medium, often yielding far more questions about what direction gaming was taking and where gamers themselves were headed next. It is my contention that video game players (gamers) and now streamers and viewers on streaming websites such as Twitch offer a crucial location for pursuing a critical inquiry into life and politics in the digital age.

I did not begin with any preconceived or narrowly defined notions of what sorts of politics or gaming I would find on the website or what sorts of "citizens" I would find there, only to investigate further into what appeared to me to be active communities exhibiting all the hallmarks of what I recognized *intuitively* to be political. I never did commit to that first streamer on his channel, but I noticed over the years how many of those around me, those old and longstanding gamer friends, inevitably did follow him on Twitch.

viii Preface

Importantly, this work is not a form of auto-ethnography. That is to say, I never considered myself fully qualified to speak from my own experience as a native to live-streaming communities. I do not count myself in the same class of gamers as the many I came to know who informed the narratives that guide this present work. This is not to say that studies that take an interest in either the familiar or home communities, or alternatively those taking a more philosophical approach engaging primarily from an established theoretical perspective, are not also perfectly legitimate; rather, I wish to offer from the outset the disclaimer that my intention was to be critically open and to explore what was, for me, completely new ground. Despite this, I do continue to call myself a gamer, even as I continue to witness those close to me migrating onto live-video streams. Informed by their participation on streams both before the start of this project and afterwards, I see this book as one of great consequence for gaming culture and for the ongoing ethnographic study of gamers who now increasingly find themselves living and forming their virtual communities in full view of significant others.

INTRODUCTION

Today, there is a great deal of anxiety over the ubiquity of the internet, large language models, generative artificial intelligence, and the "metaverse". This is true not only among scholars but across generations and in every segment of society. People are growing ever more dependent on digital technology to assist with their day-to-day tasks, everything from biodata recording to workplace and social scheduling and even, in some cases, technical aids that assist with higher-order cognitive thinking.[1] The anxiety is born from a worry about the ill-effects of spending too much time online and a fear of growing dependency on social networks and mobile devices, "doom scrolling", "tik toking" and "instagraming". There is also distress that loved ones will forget their responsibility to the world they live in, and alarm that young people, especially, are trading in their "human purpose" in favour of more "robotic moments".[2]

In this book, I explore whether gamers themselves are asking critical questions of technology as they increasingly find themselves living everyday life online, no longer spellbound in wonderment at the transformative potential of computer-mediated communication or smitten by aging promises of cyber-anonymity, fluid identities, and virtual transcendences. The consumer internet is now several decades old. If it has become ordinary, has it also become invisible? Is it beyond questioning for those who spend increasingly long periods online, participating in social networks, data clouds, quasi-legal end-user agreements, virtual workplaces, web 3.0 sociality, watching Netflix, and surfing BuzzFeed? People living their daily life in this "digital age"—gamers in particular—appear to be

DOI: 10.4324/9781003341079-1

2 Introduction

disinterested and largely oblivious to the so-called worldwide debates over the social, economic, and cultural consequences of being online. They seem more or less content with remaining permanently tethered to their mobile devices and indifferent to the various corporate and governmental organizations clandestinely surveilling and monetizing their private data. Are gamers capable of being critical? Can they be considered political?

Scholars writing in a period roughly beginning in the 2010s, when the data collection for this book began, advised that a digital generation understands and inhabits the world entirely through technology. "These days 'the social' is a feature", as Geert Lovink remarks.[3] In the view of Lovink, among others who were early on the scene for critical digital studies, the internet is jeopardizing not only a way of life but a way of thinking (and of teaching and doing research as well).[4] I argue, updating upon these earlier views, how the internet shapes morality systems in addition to social structures overrun by algorithms and artificial intelligence, by the ambitions and sometimes the radical whims of tech-CEOs and influencer gurus. Over the past decade, we have seen renewed and counterbalancing excitement once again burgeoning in the academy and among a wider public. We continue to witness celebration alongside some reticence for precisely what we continue to perceive as novel, namely the social networks that enable our sustained connectivity spanning the globe, circulating our private data at ever-accelerating speeds, enlivening or perhaps curtailing socio-political debates, and even giving birth to all new "killer apps".[5]

While many of those distrustful of the internet have now moved beyond their initial discomfort and towards a more accepting approach to interconnected life online (no less intense), scholars and the public continue to ask questions about the promise and the peril of online life. We question how we ought to navigate these domains and how best to live ethically, fairly, and with some measure of social justice in a time when reality is part digital, part social, part open source, and part corporate.[6] We are neither straightforwardly optimistic nor pessimistic, but we maintain that there is a great deal left to examine about a world that has effortlessly slid into a life lived online.[7]

In the early days of my research, interested in the lives of gamers on livestreams, I asked whether gamers exhibit forms of civic engagement in their online communities; ultimately, this question was revealed as being overly entangled in debates about the virtual/real divide. After all, "civic engagement"—an often-contested political science term traditionally rooted in the affairs of the nation-state and primarily understood in terms of official party politics—would need to capture both online and offline experiences and consider divergent concerns while simultaneously remaining relevant to gaming. I now ask not *if* gamers are political subjects but rather *how* they are political, a question indicative of their expressions, habits, and interests, which translate into actions. I am focused on an inquiry into how gamers form their own politics on live-video streams and to attend to communities, economies, inequalities, as well as transformations that occur in their day-to-day interactions.

The answers to this inquiry will surface throughout later chapters of the book, where I am attentive to the specificities of streaming culture and open to exploring what is unique about the developing relationships one finds amongst viewers and streamers in gaming. At the outset, one might rightly ask, why conceptualize the relationships between gamers and their streaming as a political issue? If streaming is political, what are the political concerns of gamers on Twitch? What gives their communities cohesion, and why should we care? In the following chapters, I build an argument about the nature of streaming as "live-video politics". I resist a dominant discourse on gamers as being disaffected, and I push back against those who would insist upon framing gamers as merely pathological or dysfunctional subjects. Indeed, I argue that streaming is not a game but a complex amalgam deserving of significantly deeper analysis than has previously surfaced from older branches of video game studies.[8] I find that if one defines a digital age as a time when perceptions of reality are increasingly viewed through the prisms of technology, where the "socio-material" is synonymous with the "socio-technical", it matters that we re-think the character of a politics to be inclusive of gamers who also inhabit the world. I submit in this book that gamers and their troubles, or indeed their triumphs, are not extraordinary or quirky phenomena beyond the purview of outsiders looking in; rather, they are significant to us all and reason enough for excitement, even inspiring hope for a brighter and more socially just digital age.[9]

Gamer or Citizen?

The starting point of my inquiry is that examining gamers requires an investigation of the gamer subject as produced politically in and through technology. That is, we ought to acknowledge how the participants described in this book are fundamentally viewed as actively productive and passively produced as members not only of the online community but simultaneously and overwhelmingly of liberal democratic societies. Gamers are undoubtedly "subjected to power" because of their media interaction in a consumer corporate society, but they are also "subjects of power" capable of and willing to actively engage in the shaping and change of the everyday lives of others. This is the foundation of what I understand as

4 Introduction

"live-video politics", but it is also an important hallmark of any complete concept of a "citizen".

As Isin and Ruppert argue in *Being Digital Citizens* (2015), cyberspace is a complex space where users become citizens, and it is through digital acts from subjects who are simultaneously "of power" and speaking "to power" that we uncover an emerging politics in a digital age.[10] Similarly, in this book, I focus on bridging the gaps in theorization between classical understandings of "politics" and "the citizen" as well as new formulations of digital rights claims that occur online in live-streams. My notion of "Gamers Citizens", like Isin and Ruppert's "Digital Citizens", emerges as the people of the live-streaming and gaming communities continue to articulate claims to a variety of things over the internet. While classical understandings of citizenship conceive of the subject as possessing rights and obligations that are bestowed by the nation-state, my critical interpretation is that the notion of "Gamer Citizen" is a vital emergent figure, one that illustrates how there are new categories of citizenship yet to be acknowledged that are negotiated as well as performed online, including but not limited to all new "political" activities: "subscribing", "stream donating", "live-chat moderating", "emoji interventions", and "hosting", among others. Moreover, these alternative enactments of citizenship ought to count alongside the fully codified classical depictions, namely "voting", "paying taxes", "attending town halls", "writing elected officials", "volunteering", "running for office", "demonstrating", "jury summons", and so on.

Key Terms: A Preliminary Discussion

In this section, I outline the key terms for this work, drawing on the relatively sparse existing literature on gamers and streamers. I outline working definitions for the following: community, streaming, politics, the digital age, online/offline, and subjects/citizens.

Community

I use the term "community" to refer to existing and coherent individual channels on Twitch, of which there were several core sites for this book, and I attach the adjective "wider" or "broader", either to reference affiliated assemblies of those channels or to stake claims about generalizable phenomena in gaming culture at large.

Live-streams on Twitch were first lauded as sites for "emergent community" that convey a sense of progress, if not a revolutionary departure, for a demonized video gaming subculture.[11] Gaming, now framed as streaming, was not simply a matter of individuals engaging with content in virtual isolation but a practice of millions of people participating together in a web environment organized for a distinctive kind of community building. These early scholars of streaming, pioneers in their own right, argue that one is enriched by streams since these are fundamentally constructive projects designed for any participant gamer. In this book, I add to this literature and investigate live-streaming on Twitch to gather a better understanding of how and why gamers find belonging and a sense of agency to build community together, all while apparently opting out of what is deemed a productive lifestyle, not only to play video games but also to become spectators of play. I consider whether arguments that gamers are disaffected youth are sufficient for understanding how live-streams emerge and how the practices we see on a live video platform can be regarded as a community.

Streaming

Twitch is a "live video platform" also known as a "video streaming service" where users can view other people playing video games or show video content relevant to video games to a global audience over the internet in real-time. This practice is generally referred to as "live-streaming" or "streaming" over channels called "streams", and I use each of these terms freely and interchangeably throughout the book. Streaming is not a new phenomenon, although there has been growing interest following advancements in internet bandwidth availability and in web video encoding and decoding technologies. Unlike other video platforms such as YouTube, where content is primarily consumed in pre-recorded format and is uploaded and subsequently viewed by audiences "on demand", live-streaming is the practice of continuous broadcasting to viewers "tuning in" from all over the world, sometimes leaving behind little or no trace for the public record.

It is apparent from the limited yet increasing work done on streaming so far that scholarly inquiries have been committed to a better understanding of the mechanics of live-streaming as a platform. That is to say, there are those who engage with the differences in feature sets that come to define websites like Twitch and how those technical tools change perceptions of video game spectatorship, redirecting attention towards gamers who now assemble in massive numbers to view gameplay online.[12] There is no shortage as well of work that begins to document new streaming tools and their influence on viewership ratings as live-streams continue to grow at exponential rates.[13] These studies do well to tell us something about how life procedurally takes shape on live-streams, but they have little more to

6 Introduction

tell us about the daily life of gamers as they stream and interact in their respective communities.

Clear to gamers and non-gamers alike who encounter streaming and Twitch for the first time is how live video offers new ways to experience gameplay.[14] Pablo Cesar and David Geerts offer to this day a most precise and helpful categorization of the technology that drives streaming platforms in their framing of "social TV". Building upon earlier attempts to theorize the medium, they trace a fundamental shift in how people interact with what was traditionally understood as television content and socialize through four new activity categories:[15] "(1) Content selection and sharing where information by other peers is used for making decisions on what to watch; (2) Communication which may take the form of direct communication via chat, audio or video with other peers; (3) Community building by commenting about a program with a large community; and (4) Status updates making available to others what you are currently watching".[16] Each of these characteristics is visible on Twitch, and indeed, many of them are features to be interrogated in the forthcoming chapters of this book. Yet these tools, which Cesar and Geerts maintain qualify a medium as a form of social TV, are not necessarily novel nor, in large part, a departure from assemblies in other offline settings where people search, share, and spread the word based on their unique and varied interests.[17] Indeed, media communities are found wherever fellowship and cohabitation are made possible and are currently rendered through some form of mediation.[18]

Nevertheless, a few have asked the question, "does live-video streaming change the (video) game?" Of course, what these tools accomplish for gamers and how they might relate to politics and a world beyond gaming cannot be revealed solely through conceptual clarifications and technological formulations on how streaming is similar to or different from television. The Twitch literature up to now has posed many sorts of different questions going further into the actual practices of gamers on stream, but I argue they do not go far enough. In *Watch Me Playing, I am a Professional: a First Study on Video Game Live Streaming*, Kaytoue et al. ask how "electronic-sport" (E-Sport)—a competitive format on Twitch—is a growing and popular commercial activity. Kaytoue, hoping to bring to light a particular culture of streaming, seeks, through an analysis of Esports, to gain the attention of industrial partners.[19] Although there are several moments of discovery where new kinds of relationships between streamer and viewer arise in this exploratory work—for instance, in an outlier case, a continuous stream was found running for 97 days as part of a group of gamers running a marathon—these were ultimately assembled to make space for an analysis of how streaming functions in order to become more profitable for game producers and streamer businesses.[20] Similarly, in another study titled *E-Sports on the*

Rise?: Critical Considerations on the Growth and Erosion of Organized Digital Gaming Competitions, Witkowski et al. ask how best to conceptualize Esports at the intersection of gaming and sport on live-streams.[21] Though we have the word critical in the title, what counts within this consideration of streamer culture is again framed within the limited scope of new sporting possibilities, competition, and, chiefly, commercial success. While these early characterizations and explorations do answer previous calls from research communities within the information sciences to understand game spectatorship on streams as they propel the games industry, they focus exclusively on the sole category of Esports and offer little in terms of a deeper understanding of gamers' lives and daily practices in the community.[22]

This is *not* a book focused on the features or qualities of live-video as a central object of study; rather, it is one that seeks a wider social and political understanding of gamers as active subjects in their community live-streams. To clarify, streaming is not the object of analysis in this book; rather, it is a means of analysis in pursuit of greater clarification on the core inquiry— namely to explore the politics of/for "Gamer Citizens".

Politics and the Digital Age

I define the present moment in history as a digital age precisely because it is a time when we increasingly cannot even comprehend a socio-material existence, a daily life, outside of our use of technology and the internet. Raymond Williams, an important scholar to consider for any work that aims to challenge received understandings of "culture" and "politics" of the everyday, argues across several of his most influential texts that an analysis of society has to be concerned with the "real social context of our economic and political life" in tandem with the indissoluble aspects of "real communities living in their valuably various ways".[23] Britain in the 1960s, as Williams understands it, was undergoing a rapid transformation in which cultural forms were shifting towards a model based on mass production and a consumer society. For Williams, this shift presented a problem that was not simply political and social in nature but also a practical issue for education. A consumer society is a "confused society" in which people are no longer learning to challenge the exceptionally complicated process of a dominant capitalist social order, one that imposes a hegemony and is especially neglectful, excluding, repressing, or simply failing to recognize the qualities of a "practical consciousness".[24] Socio-material life in Williams' time—a precursor to the digital age—was fuelled by "inferior and destructive elements" propagated on television, in magazines, and in literature as well as music. Together, these were seen to restrict the development of artistic, creative, and democratic freedoms alike.[25]

8 Introduction

Culture is ordinary, Williams famously argues (1958),[26] but this is not intended to assert that one form of culture should succeed over another. Rather, in every society and in every age, people mark out "a whole way of life" that is a blending of the traditional and the creative in daily life. For Williams, "culture" is, in practice, "politics" by another name, an understanding that does not diminish the integrity of either concept but instead implies that neither idiom is strong enough to ever escape the purview of the other. Thus, the challenge for a study of culture *and* politics is to understand how these two meanings must coexist and to resist the urge that is born of residual and powerful traditions, institutions, and formations that require and enforce a clear separation between the two terms.

I thus places special emphasis on social processes of a constitutive kind. Culture and politics of the everyday offer a different sense of human growth and development—crucially born of historical materialism—that offers a criticism of and an alternative to "civilization" and "civil society" as fixed and achieved conditions.[27] There are, however, several perennial problems. For instance, if we recognize the indivisible connections between material production, politics, culture, and everyday activity, how, for the sake of analysis can we track causation between events in different areas? Which "elements" or "productive forces" can be said to be determining, and which are determined? Alternatively, phrased in Williams' own terms, how can the "emergent" ever triumph over the "dominant" or the "residual"? Williams' answer, through a perhaps vague conjoining of terms, is that we can distinguish "structures of feeling", namely values and meanings that are actively lived and felt and which come to form systems at the intersection between social life and ordinary personal experience.[28] As Michael E. Gardiner indicates in *Critiques of everyday life* (2000), there is a whole host of theorizations about everyday life occurring and continuing into the 21st century that expand on the idea of structures of feeling. Exemplary work in this direction includes the French tradition of everyday life theorizing from the Surrealists to Henri Lefebvre, Agnes Heller and the connections between everyday rationality and ethics, and Dorothy E. Smith's feminist perspectives on the everyday.[29]

Finally, I define politics in this work as relations of power in the affairs of people living everyday life in a community. "Live-video politics", a key finding and conclusion to this book, is a complex of those relations between gamers living and producing culture daily in a digital age on Twitch, where they grow and develop according to a complex of inner and external processes. Importantly, this politics manifests at the nexus of online and offline.

Online and Offline

If we are witnessing a phenomenon of social TV in streaming, it is both social and television because of a complete blending of the sociality that came before it, a medium that today knows no divisions between online and offline.

It is helpful at this juncture to outline further what this book does *not* attempt to accomplish. As already stipulated, this is not an inquiry that seeks greater clarification on the form and function of streaming, nor is it an investigation of how live-streaming is broadly changing the face of gaming as a cultural form. The role of internet communication technologies (ICT) in shaping society, of which streaming is increasingly a popular activity yet equally encompasses a variety of related areas such as "big data", privacy, and security, is ambiguous at best. The internet is commonly coopted in support of metanarratives of liberation, grand theories of progress, or, alternatively, as part of a critical damnation for its corrupting influence and inculcation of unwholesome values. Manuel Castells offers that internet communication technologies assimilate social institutions and subsume human consciousness—even bodies—into the flow of an information society, a "network of networks".[30] While more recent accounts may appear less rhetorical, it is still apparent in contemporary thought that there persists a focus on individual agency, critical thinking, social justice, and concerns for the integrity of social relationships, as these are seen to be heavily implicated problems of/for the internet. I do not deny that there are important challenges, indeed even vital concerns, to the future of a digital age in taking a techno-sceptical view, but I do not principally aim to contribute answers to questions on the dichotomy of the material and virtual world. I do not probe further into debates of online versus offline or resolve the incompatibilities between cyberspace and physical space. Rather, I begin from the position that it is fruitful to suspend the division between online and offline, focusing instead on the communities that develop with new technologies.

Angela Crack rightly indicates that "the role of ICT [internet communication technology] in world politics and society is ambiguous: It helps to bolster the prevailing order *and* allows contradictions in the status quo to be exploited by counterhegemonic forces".[31] Marianne Franklin builds on this premise to identify how the internet is often found in scholarly literature to be socially determining as well as organizationally and theoretically overdetermined.[32] Franklin finds that: (1) there are clear preferences for "state centric" studies where political science and international relations form a large part of internet governance; (2) research is commonly "media centric", delving deeply into the everyday or strategic

10 Introduction

uses of the web for social ends. These call chiefly upon similarities and distinctions between different mediums (i.e. film, social media, virtual reality); (3) scholarship can be classified as "techno centric" where research covers technologies and the dynamics of design; and finally, (4) an emerging literature that reveals the problematics of network design, infrastructure, and popular usage with growing concerns for geo-political and economic consequences, for example, private corporations governing the underlying internet operation and open source/open access in addition to internet human rights and responsibilities.[33] Franklin is careful in *Digital Dilemmas: Power, Resistance, and the Internet* (2013) not to (re)create "either/or" claims that insist on choosing one side in favour of offline or online manifestations. In this regard, both Franklin and Crack share the goal of initiating a normative shift towards an emphasis on the "how" and equally the "who" of internet studies. Their efforts are consistent with trends in video game studies where, for instance, Garry Crawford asserts that what is actually required is to put an end to our fixation on video games as central objects of study and to move to the study of gamers themselves—players who offer a deeper understanding of the study of video games, key aspects of play, gamer culture, and everyday life.[34]

On the meaning of online/offline within the context of live-streaming on Twitch, this book therefore offers only working definitions. As will become more apparent throughout, other scholars have already proposed a plethora of working definitions of their own: "video game space", "platform", "magic circles", "frames", "LANscapes", "Human Activity Systems", and "lifeworlds". While I argue that these concepts are/can be useful, they are often mistakenly taken up as paramount. They supersede any focus on gamer subjects as primary. The concepts lead us to focus on the platforms as spaces rather than on the lives of gamers as people living in communities. With a focus on politics and everyday life, we can end the cycle of theorizing platforms in place of social forms. Importantly, the gamers in this book themselves spend little time pondering the essence of worlds apart. Instead, they search for a place within streaming to call their own.

Navigating the Text

This book consists of a series of chapters that delve into case studies from contemporary gaming and live-streaming. At several intersections, the reader will encounter various comprehension tools. These tools appear as follows in each chapter:

Introduction **11**

CLOSE-UP: "CONCEPT A"

"Close-ups" are pop-up bubbles clarifying for the reader the definition and function of secondary terms. It is important to consider these definitions as working concepts since they might also have alternative meanings in other fields/studies.

ACTIVITY

There will be several learner activities throughout the book. These activities are intended to give the reader pause and encourage reflection on the arguments presented.

QUESTIONS

At the end of each chapter, there are a series of comprehension questions. It is a good idea to attempt to answer a few of these questions before progressing to subsequent chapters.

Notes

1 Here I am referring to the use of digital assistants like Amazon's Alexa, Google's Assistant, and Apple's Siri to help make decisions, for example, recall destinations visited recently based on personal map data, state important facts about the world or current events local to you, and even assist with food shopping and cooking based on current supplies in the home.
2 Turkle, S. (2011). Alone Together: Why We Expect More from Technology and Less from Each Other. Basic Books: New York, 19.
3 Lovink, Geert (2011). Networks Without a Cause: A Critique of Social Media. Polity Press: Cambridge, 6.
4 Kroker, Arthur. (2013). Critical Digital Studies. University of Toronto Press.
5 For "Spanning the globe" reference, see the following recent books which offer a renewed focus on social media connectivity: Werbach, K. (2020). After

12 Introduction

the Digital Tornado: Networks, Algorithms, Humanity. Cambridge University Press; Teens, Screens, and Social Connection: An Evidence-Based Guide to Key Problems and Solutions. (2023). Germany: Springer International Publishing; and Roy, S. (2021). Social Media and Capitalism: People, Communities and Commodities. Canada: Daraja Press; For "ever accelerating speeds," see: Wajcman, Judy (2014). Pressed for Time: The Acceleration of Life in Digital Capitalism. Chicago: University of Chicago Press; for "socio-political debates," see Social Media News and Its Impact. (2021). United Kingdom: Taylor & Francis; for "killer apps," see Packer, J., Reeves, J. (2020). Killer Apps: War, Media, Machine. United Kingdom: Duke University Press.

6 See: Dyer-Witheford N. (2015). Cyber-Proletariat: Global Labour in the Digital Vortex. London: Pluto Press. See also for developments in Virtual Reality: L. Nakamura, "Feeling Good about Feeling Bad: Virtuous Virtual Reality and the Automation of Racial Empathy," Journal of Visual Culture 19, no. 1 (2020): 47–64.

7 Turkle, S. (2015). Reclaiming Conversation: The Power of Talk in a Digital Age. Penguin Books.

8 Anderson, C.A., & Bushman. B.J. (2001) "Effects of violent video games on aggressive behavior, aggressive cognition, aggressive affect, physiological arousal, and prosocial behavior: A meta-analytical review of the scientific literature". Psychological Science, 12, 353–359; and Lee, Kwan Min; Peng, Wei (2009), "What Do We Know About Social and Psychological Effects of Computer Games? A Comprehensive Review of the Current Literature" in Playing Video Games: Motives, Responses, and Consequences, Vorderer, Peter and Jennings Bryant (eds): Taylor & Francsis e-Library.

9 See the following books for a "darker" more pessimistic view of the digital age: Morozov, Evgeny (2011). The Net Delusion: The Dark Side of Internet Freedom. Public Affairs: New York; and Bartlett, Jamie (2014) The Dark Net: Inside the Digital Underworld. William Heinemann: London.

10 Isin, Engin. & Evelyn Ruppert (2015) Being Digital Citizens. Rowman & Littlefield Publishing Group.

11 Kaytoue, M., Silva, A., Cerf, L., Meira Jr, W., & Raïssi, C. (2012). "Watch me playing, I am a professional: a first study on video game live streaming". In Proceedings of the 21st International Conference Companion on World Wide Web (pp. 1181–1188). ACM; Hamilton, W. A., Garretson, O., & Kerne, A. (2014). "Streaming on twitch: fostering participatory communities of play within live mixed media". In Proceedings of the 32nd Annual ACM Conference on Human Factors in Computing Systems (pp. 1315–1324). ACM.

12 For early examples see: Chorianopoulos, K., and Lekakos, G. 2007. "Learn and play with interactive TV". Entertainment Computing 5, 2; Bruns, A. 2009. "The user-led disruption: self-(re)broadcasting". In Proceedings of the Seventh European Conference on European Interactive Television Conference (EuroITV '09). ACM, New York, NY, USA, 87–90; Basapur, S., Mandalia, H., Chaysinh, S., Lee, Y., Venkitaraman, N., and Metcalf, C. (2012). "FANFEEDS: evaluation of socially generated information feed on second screen as a TV show companion." In Proceedings of the 10th European Conference on Interactive TV and Video (EuroiTV '12). ACM, New York, NY, USA, 87–96.

13 For early examples see: Xiao, Yang & Xioajiang Du (2007), "Internet Protocol Television (IPTV): The Killer Application For the Next-Generation Internet." In Rochester Institute of Technology RIT Scholar Works IEEE Communications Magazine, November 2007; Shin, Dong-Hee (2013). "Defining

Sociability and Social Presence in Social TV". Computers in Human Behavior 29 (2013) 939–947.

14 For early examples see: Cesar, P., & Geerts, D. (2011). "Past, present, and future of social TV: a categorization". In Consumer Communications and Networking Conference (CCNC), 2011 IEEE (pp. 347–351). IEEE; Shin, Dong-Hee (2013). "Defining Sociability and Social Presence in Social TV". Computers in Human Behavior 29 (2013) 939–947; Coppens, Toon, Liieven Trappeniers, Marc Godon (2004). "AmigoTV: Towards a Social TV Experience" in Alcatel Bell RI Residential Networked Applications Francis Wellesplein. Antwerp Belgium.

15 Early research by Chorianopoulos and Harboe raise questions about the transition from a unidirectional form of distributed content to multidirectional or bidirectional channels of communication. In many ways, this work was prescient of the future of live-video streaming, however, more focused on the sharing and discussion of traditional television, movies and music. See Chorianopoulos, K. (2007). "Content Enriched Communication With Interactive TV". The Journal of Communications Network, 6(1):23–30; Harboe, G. (2009). "In Search of Social Television." In Geerts D and Chorianopoulos, K. (eds). Social Interactive Television: Immersive Experiences and Perspectives. IGI Global.

16 Cesar. P & Geerts, D, "Past, present, and future of social TV", 2.

17 See: Morley, D. (1997). Television, Audiences and Cultural Studies. London: Routledge.

18 See: Hipfl, B. & Theo Hug Eds (2006). Media Communities. Waxmann Verlag: Germany.

19 Kaytoue, M., Silva, A., Cerf, L., Meira Jr, W., & Raïssi, C. (2012). "Watch me playing, I am a professional: a first study on video game live streaming". In Proceedings of the 21st International Conference Companion on World Wide Web (pp. 1181–1188). ACM.

20 Kaytoue, M., Silva, A., Cerf, L., Meira Jr, W., & Raïssi, C. (2012), 1185.

21 Witkowski, E., Hutchins, B., & Carter, M. (2013). "E-sports on the rise?: Critical considerations on the growth and erosion of organized digital gaming competitions". In Proceedings of the 9th Australasian Conference on Interactive Entertainment: Matters of Life and Death (p. 43). ACM.

22 Cheung, Gifford and Jeff Huang (2011). "Starcraft from the stands: understanding the game spectator". Proceeding CHI '11 Proceedings of the SIGCHI Conference on Human Factors in Computing Systems, 763–772.

23 Williams, R. (1965). The long revolution. Orchard Park, NY: Broadview Press, 363.

24 Williams, R. (1973). Marxism and literature. Oxford: Oxford University Press, 125.

25 Williams, R. (1965). The long revolution. Orchard Park, NY: Broadview Press, 365.

26 Williams, R. (1965). 365.

27 Williams, "Marxism and Literature", 14.

28 Williams, "Marxism and Literature", 131.

29 Gardiner, M.E. (2000). Critiques of Everyday Life. Routledge: London.

30 Castells, Manuel (1996) The Rise of the Network Society: Rise of the Network Society. Oxford: Blackwell, 2000.

31 Crack, Angela M. (2008). Global Communication and Transnational Public Spheres. New York: Palgrave Macmillan, 2.

32 Franklin, M.I. (2013) Digital Dilemmas: Power, Resistance and the Internet. Oxford: Oxford University Press, 37.

33 Franklin, "Digital Dilemmas", 42.

34 Crawford, G (2012). Video Gamers. London: Routledge.

1

A POLITICS OF BEING GAMERS

Introduction

What is the politics of being a gamer? There are a few in contemporary game studies who have, for the most part, rejected the widespread pathologizing of gamers as disaffected. Their research now aims to reflect more responsibly on video games and to investigate gamers as individuals with flourishing social followings and subjectivities that are considerably more complex and multidimensional than were previously assumed. On this branch of research, however, we are still locked at the centre of an aging debate where, on the one side, conservative reformers continue to take aim at "violent" and "anti-social" video games for corrupting youth and inculcating unwholesome values, and on the other extreme, scholars, who are often video game enthusiasts themselves, come to form a band of academics working in defence of positivity in gaming, viewing gamers as uniquely praiseworthy. One could argue that video games are violent, causing damaging media effects on young gamers who cannot adequately separate their virtual from actual personas; alternatively, one could make a more responsible critical analysis of gamers as they ought to be framed, more independent of the manifest representations of violent video games. Either way, with few exceptions, video games and gamers who play them have been predominantly understood—not only in the mainstream but also within the burgeoning academic literature—as quirky and part of extraordinary and often dangerous affiliations. What is more, gamers continue to be studied and viewed as though they must stand in binary opposition to important signifiers of the prevailing social democratic order. Thus, the

DOI: 10.4324/9781003341079-2

politics of being a gamer is the politics of building community in defiance of disaffection. It is a politics of continuing to find engagements beyond virtual worlds, occasionally in service of grandiose goals like gathering support for a presidential election, or challenging the prevailing policy of a government, or even helping to end a brutal and unjust war. Often, however, the politics of being a gamer is chiefly about carrying on living as a gamer through these troubled times. Simply put, the politics of being a gamer is the politics first and foremost of gaming in this digital age.

In this chapter, I provide a theoretical frame for understanding the complex social and political ethos that we might call "gamer politics", or the politics of being gamers. This is to seek out new openings for video game studies beyond the now-aging and mired debates over how the medium functions as a corrupting force in the lives of young people. Can gamers be considered citizens? Is the gamer subject antithetical to the citizen subject? How might these figures co-exist or collide? Is there room in the theoretical landscape for a "Gamer Citizen"? U.S. House Representative Alexandria Ocasio-Cortez (AOC) appears to hold out some hope that we might soon find answers to these questions. In the summer of 2020, she started her own live-streaming channel on Twitch as an attempt to get out the vote for the United States presidential elections. Her efforts culminated in a collaborative series of live video streams alongside other popular streamers such as Pokimane and HasanAbi, broadcasting community game play in a massively popular video game at the time, *Among Us*.[1] There was significant social media content generation in this effort aimed at unlocking the voting potential of gamers, including an image designed using video game assets for the event to generate excitement for the more than one million subscribers who gathered to watch AOC play. Being the first congresswoman of colour to participate in a video game event of this kind, her success at drawing massive viewership numbers not only serves as evidence of an enlivened gamer community surrounding traditional politics but also signifies an opening for gamers to find all new progressive agency in following a politician like AOC, leveraging their digital activity for tangible election-day results. Following suit, Twitch as a platform itself decided to deploy its profoundly popular Kappa emoji to launch their own "Don't Lurk on Democracy!" campaign (Figure 1.1).[2] In a similar fashion, this initiative was intended to drive interest amongst Twitch youth, to encourage viewers to vote in the 2020 presidential election, and to address a clear and present need for the live-streaming platform to generate engagement beyond the confines of virtual worlds and video games.[3] If not a calling for "civic responsibility" in gamers, these examples of outreach at the very least signal renewed leadership, marking out through partnerships in streaming the playful breaking of boundaries between worlds.[4]

FIGURE 1.1   This illustrated example uses the Statue of Liberty featured prominently alongside the Kappa Emoji in her torch, sourced from Twitch marketing materials. The poster was created to raise awareness for the 2020 U.S. presidential election. (Twitch, 2020)

A politics of being gamers must initially be read amidst this recent backdrop, notably a context that is firmly anchored chiefly in the United States within a mythos of migration and the virtues of democracy in the nation-state. Continuing in the American context, gamers do not always so favorably translate their energies into what might be deemed as acceptable "civic activity". What counts as suitable in "politics" is always a matter of contention, yet on Twitch gamers continue to participate in a manner that is firmly dedicated to virtual worlds; this is in stark opposition to concerns from the perceived exterior world, a realm for which many gamers feel no affinity, considering it to be outside the purview of gaming. As Patricia Hernandez reports:

> No matter whose Twitch stream you're on, there are a few unwritten rules that you can reliably expect to be enforced. You shouldn't spam in the chat. You shouldn't advertise someone else's stream. You should be nice. You should speak the same language as everyone else. And, more often than not: You shouldn't bring up politics ... On Twitch, talking about politics can be taboo ... streamers tend to avoid *certain* topics.[5]

Overtly "political" topics like voting and campaigning are opposed on Twitch almost as vehemently as other forms of undesirable speech, yet traditional political interests never disappear completely from the platform.[6] As a sizable voting segment, gamers present a perhaps too tantalizing prize, and we continue to see political representatives broadcasting in a concerted effort to capture the loyalties of a new generation. Paradoxically, all this is to build inroads with a userbase that ostensibly understands their platform as a politics-free zone.[7]

Each of these moments of state-political ingress is a reflection and a more fundamental challenge to our lack of understanding over what ought to count as a legitimate part of gaming, either as a cultural or political form. Developments in activity on Twitch also test how gamers respond when they find themselves caught up over competing power struggles that were priorly held as exterior to cherished virtual worlds. Certainly, video games and gamer communities have emerged as sites of protest on Twitch, and this has come to enable, elaborate, and represent activist movements, sometimes unsettling large game studios and at times even rallying against the official policies of local and national governments. What is more, "gamer politics", or the politics of being gamers, has found expression beyond solely an American geo-political perspective, blossoming across the globe as mobilizing gamers use their live streams as a catalyst for change. For example, in Hong Kong, leveraging the spatial politics of play, gamers have protested the injustice of an eroding democracy. At center stage in this "umbrella movement" there is an Esports gaming community wherein a competitive champion from the video game Hearthstone named Blizchung shouted "Liberate Hong Kong, revolution of our age!" at his now infamous victory speech broadcast without sanction on Twitch.[8] Political activation is also emerging from community groups in Brazil, where gamers on Twitch have been clear indicators of changing societal attitudes and shifts in government policies aimed at controlling the population's sexual orientation. Commonly, Twitch has served as a positive content hub for "LGBTQ+" communities, hosting gamers to address the political struggles of minority groups.[9] In Brazil, however, a contingent calling themselves "gaymers" is pushing past stereotypes in a concerted effort to resist serious injustices from multiple sides in their home country—namely from far-right wing nationalist government policies that suppress the freedoms of same-sex couples as well as fuel an ongoing cycle of violence.[10] Lastly, we now routinely witness the phenomenon of "gaming for good" (see Chapter 3), charity gaming, and streaming events, which have frequented Twitch since its earliest days as a live service.

In 2022, gamers from around the globe raised $36 million in just 24 hours of fundraising in support of war-torn Ukraine. Gamers assembled on Twitch to raise funds to assist survivors, thereby staking a clear and principled stance against what they perceived to be an unjust and brutal invasion.[11] Each of these examples is a confirmation that any complete

18 A Politics of Being Gamers

notion of "politics" must also include the ability to challenge the prevailing powers and dominant social orders of nation-states. Inarguably, gamers from around the world do participate "politically" by leveraging their streaming communities on Twitch in massive numbers.

This chapter takes on the following trajectory. First, I focus on gamers and the social and cultural significance of gaming as paramount. This is to present the idea that there is a movement from disaffection to engagement. Next, I consider a few perspectives from the area of citizenship studies to suggest that the internet and democracy, young citizens, and "civic play", further complicate not just a discussion of digital divides but also a political divide for gamers. Gamers are assumed to be "learner citizens" and are perceived as far from ideal political subjects, thus preventing a complete emergence from disaffection. Following, I argue how space remains central to an understanding of gaming and gamers. In these contemporary works, the video game constitutes a special moment in time and space sustained by a logic of the "magic circle" that both circumscribes and encloses. There is tension and often a split focus between the video game as the object of study and the gamer subject as a key node of enquiry, and these sustain a theoretical block preventing any discussion of gamers as political. To set up a foundation for the analysis forthcoming in the rest of the book, I close the chapter by offering a few working premises describing the politics of being gamers and the emerging figure that I call "Gamer Citizen".

Dominant Discourses on Disaffection

What I call "the dominant discourse of disaffection" (DDD) draws its roots and finds a legacy in behavioural psychology. For an explanation of this important phenomenon, I turn to Lt. Col. Dave Grossman, a retired military psychologist and media effects researcher who minces no words in his book, later co-authored with revisions from Gloria DeGaetano, titled *Stop Teaching Our Kids to Kill*.[12] This work builds on a longer list of similar publications calling to action not only other scholars but also parents, policy makers, and mental health practitioners against video game violence; depictions of violence in older television and movie mass media outlets are also implicated in a broader epidemic that is allegedly priming "children to see killing as acceptable".[13] Though appearing late in the argument, there are references to studies that draw a causal link between the brutalization that occurs on screen with classical conditioning, operant conditioning, and role modelling, yet there is little regard, if any at all, towards the primary assumptions underlying the critique. For instance, not very much is up for debate when it comes to unpacking the meaning of "harm" in cases of violent video games. What is more, we are meant to understand gaming not as any sort of productive cultural form—for better or for worse—but rather as a damaging "habit".

Gaming is seen as a steady "diet" of violent entertainment that, when left unchecked, ultimately leads without much deviation towards addiction, to violence, and finally to criminality. For Grossman, there can be no doubt that many criminals copy crimes they see represented in the media, reproducing violent sprees in gruesome detail and with "cold-blooded" calculation. Gamer disaffection, or the DDD as I come to understand it, emerges from this primary logic of pathology, wherein a gamer's psyche invariably comes to form a relationship to unhealthy media consumption and to video games, ultimately shutting out the wider world and all the people who form a necessary part of it.

As I explore in later chapters, from the perspective of the dominant discourse, gamer "community", "togetherness", and "politics" never enter the core discussion. Most alarmingly, the DDD imposes not only a "culture of cruelty" and separation for an alleged few, whose indifference builds to violence, but it also establishes a fundamental abnormality in all people who may identify as gamers.[14] In the cultural mainstream, all gamers (not only would be killers) are understood to develop an inability to engage socially; it is not only sensationalized texts, viz., Grossman and DeGaetano, but also more reputable academic texts—even textbooks—that fuel this problematic discourse. Richard Jackson Harris and Fred W. Sanborn, authors of *Cognitive Psychology of Mass Communication*, present their arguments now in a *6th edition*. They note that "probably the most common general perspective in studying the media is a search for the 'effects' of exposure to mass communication … These effects can be direct, conditional, or cumulative".[15] Such models emphasize a self-defeating understanding of human psychology. It is not simply that the psyche is an insignificant unit of study or that we gain nothing from exploring the real detriments of mental health disorders. Importantly, behavioural psychology presents demonstrable advantages in cases where people do encounter hardship in connection with their gaming activities, as we shall examine more closely throughout this book, but there are, in addition and more profoundly, further consequences to the default pathological view of gamers. Through dogged determination to present the case of illness, poor mental health, and media violence ahead of all other perspectives, that side effect is to imbue a dominant discourse on gamers as disaffected, presenting a world that is mostly hostile and adversarial towards gaming.

The DDD, as we shall see, brings with it far more harmful ill effects than helpful remedies, as proponents who deploy this language borrow from behavioural psychology and condemn young gamers for their affliction of playing video games. Gamers invariably, whether consciously or

20 A Politics of Being Gamers

not, view their gaming as fundamentally damaging. What is more, this **discourse** serves to poison relationships between non-gamers and gamers alike, spreading interpersonal malaise in all sorts of peripheral contact zones such as performance in school, security of employment, physical health, and even in romantic relationships.

CLOSE-UP 1: "DISCOURSE"

In large part, we give meaning to all our experiences in life and to each of our encounters with others through frameworks of language. As media and cultural theorist Stuart Hall remarked, "language, in this sense, is a signifying practice".[16] This practice gives rise not only to our ability to negotiate the everyday routines of social life but also, critically, provides a platform from which to approach the effects and consequences of political life. "Discourse" means not only communication of your thought by words, talk, and conversation, but it fundamentally equates to language that has grown cohesive enough to produce specific knowledge, i.e., meaning that connects to **power**, to the regulation of **conduct**, and to the construction of **identities** and **subjectivities**. Dominant discourses, therefore, fundamentally shape the way certain things are represented, debated, practiced, and even studied.

In response, it is important to avoid the pitfalls of the DDD and shift the terms of discussion towards a focus on video game players themselves. This in turn is necessitated by virtue of the rapidly trending communication paradigms of live video streaming on platforms like Twitch that go beyond traditional gameplay. From this base, we can interpret the narrative scripts and stories that are revealed in the field as one engages in participant observation with gamers in their community channels. The moments represented in the forthcoming analysis illustrate the need to go beyond commonplace bounds of acceptability and to challenge through a critical inquiry all notions of the unacceptable or disaffected gamer; this is not to release gamers from accountability but rather to hold them to account as functional citizens in a digital age.

Lately, there has been a notable shift in scholarly attention towards developing frameworks about gamers that reveal them as people who are socially significant and worthy of serious study, if not high regard. At the same time, the internet, democracy, and young citizenship, together with gaming, have come to form a dialectic of vital concern regarding the ongoing health and future of politics in our digital age. These intersections for gamers, namely between the socio-ethnographic study of their virtual activity and contemporary political commentary about their inherently troubled youth, continue to be implicated in a wider problematic they also face—that is, a persistent repudiation towards their sense of self-worth as productive subjects and a moral indignation towards their primary medium of engagement and social contact, video games. Gamers, now overwhelmingly forming a group that is condemned for its waywardness, will paradoxically soon be called upon for our technological salvation as inheritors of the incumbent democracy. As such, it is my aim here, in this first chapter, to establish the following chief operational claim that will find openings throughout the book: There exists, alive and well, a DDD on gamers, a discourse that presents those who draw a significant proportion of their sociability and identity from video games as fundamentally disaffected from politics and other important affairs of the "real" world.

From Disaffection to Engagement

Gamers are significant beyond their alleged disfunction. Much as others within the broader scope of critical digital studies have recently begun to argue, a few in a group of scholars under the smaller umbrella of video game studies have routinely contested the view that either video games or the information technology platforms that sustain their virtual worlds constitute a separate domain from a "real" life for gamers.[17] We can study the life-worlds of gaming and lay the intellectual groundwork for a study on the gamer community, but this requires that we attend to realities in the daily material life of people who play video games.[18] In their edited collection *Online Gaming in Context: The Social and Cultural Significance of Online Gaming* (2011),[19] editors Garry Crawford, Ben Light, and Victoria K. Gosling offer an ambitious yet enduringly relevant collection of key debates exploring the extent to which gamers constitute a social world that is supportive of representational, ludic, and communal aspects that span many important situated contexts. None of the 22 scholars featured in this volume argue that video games are distinct and separate from the material conditions on which they are built and depend. Instead, topics—which include old favourites such as the nature of virtual communities, online empowerment, and consumption, as well as studies of identities, language, productivity, aesthetics, and social exclusions—are found to bridge the virtual and the material. The writers in this collection explore the stories and lives of gamers themselves as well as their actual circumstances of gameplay, all this in vital consideration of gaming as a key cultural form for the 21st century.

22 A Politics of Being Gamers

There are several avenues by which to bring gamers into sharper focus. The first is to acknowledge where video games have had clear economic consequences. Video game currencies (existing long before anyone ever uttered the word "bitcoin", "NFT", or "crypto") have been in circulation and will continue to hold value in direct trade with U.S. dollars well into the foreseeable future.[20] Indeed, in *World of Warcraft*, an often-cited example and one at the centre of much theory as well as some stern criticism, gamers continue to make use of in-game gold that is also made available and sold at auction houses for real-money transactions. This has profited gamers individually and has generated entire communities that are less focused on narrative scripts and gameplay mechanics, inclined instead to follow their own profit-motive.[21] On the other hand, we have seen reason to remain critical of these upstarts, observing not only the positive growth of the video game industry and its multifaceted landscape ripe for monetary exploitation but also exploring the convergence of gaming technology with nefarious capital interests. As technological advancements herald promises for democratization through the economic liberation of a select few gamers, it is important to underscore the darker "underbelly" of this evolution, namely the exploitation and alienation of a new workforce within a vast digital economy serving to reenforce age-old class inequality.[22]

If one finds economic theory unconvincing, there are other, perhaps softer, yet no less pertinent avenues to explore. Video games present gamers with more uncommon yet tangible opportunities to extend their play into the lives of others. We can, for instance, remark on the benefits of alternative realities, which create actual opportunities to address real-world challenges and enhance human well-being. Video games can satisfy genuine human needs that the outside world is currently unable to adequately address—meaningful friendship or constructive collaborations, for instance—and ultimately offer fundamental principles from game play that can be applied to positive societal change. Jane McGonigal notes poignantly how "game design isn't just a technological craft. It's a twenty-first-century way of thinking and leading. And gameplay isn't just a pastime. It's a twenty-first-century way of working together to accomplish real change".[23]

It is from a growing online context, a foundational base that serves scholars and non-specialists alike, that gaming as a social and cultural form has been seen to flourish in many ways. We ought, though, to be careful to note that the current "state of play" should also be read in vital consideration of a long history of gaming where gamer communities have long since exhibited similar ties as they have assembled "in real life" (irl) for many decades. In fact, gamers have gathered to play video games together since the earliest days, when they were still called "electronic amusements". Gaming has offered human contacts and a source of kinship, in addition to other more solitary machine–human social relations, since as early as the 1950s.[24] When taken together, this culminates in a fundamental disruption to the idea of the recent moral panic over the disaffected gamer.

ACTIVITY 1

Pause for a moment and think about some of the settings in which you might find yourself playing video games. How many dimensions are there to this game? Focus on some examples, perhaps from your own experiences or maybe drawing from the experiences of a parent, relative, friend, or child close to you. What scholarly questions or concerns arise when we shift our focus to video games, gamers, and gaming in this new light. What happens when we move our analysis from disaffection towards alternative engagements?

The need to explore gaming in a new light and to reveal the social and cultural significance of video games is an imperative that many scholars take on. The texts available represent a clear turn in the literature towards the sociological study of gamers that has seen a response in kind from others taking an ethnographic approach, illuminating the concerns of these hybrid environments. Helen Thornham adds her detailed ethnographic account to a select group of online anthropologists who strive to map the trends and behaviours of gaming to better depict a household context.[25] In looking at 11 homes where gamers reside and observing their playing habits over a four-year period, Thornham renders a remarkably complex picture. Having spent considerable time in the field, she reveals a complex relationship between gamers and a cohesive gamer identity. She notes how gameplay preferences differ significantly across time and also migrate onto newer video game devices, yet there are traceable attitudes and characteristics of play that persist despite evolutions in game development and hardware. Among several surprise findings, for example, girls and women not only play video games but also consistently excel at several of them, on occasion holding higher scores than their male in-house counterparts.[26] Girls and boys, men and women alike, however, expressed significant sensitivity to revealing themselves and their gamer identities for fear of encountering the preconceptions and panics they associate with non-gamers from the outside looking in. Ethnographic work

24 A Politics of Being Gamers

of this kind challenges the now-aging debates about male/female player divides while also signalling a need to be critical of the wider issue of gamer discrimination and vilification that is experienced across gaming communities.[27]

We move then towards a focus on gamers as multidimensional as well as multidetermined subjects. This is now fast becoming an established analytic, not just that video games are more than their constitutive code but also that gamers who play amount to more than mere by-products of their associated activities—that is to say, gamers are increasingly viewed as post-modern subjects with considerable agency and a will to resist the flow of dominant discourses.[28]

Nevertheless, much of this perspective remains in its formative stages. While we might readily accept and even excitedly align with studies of a similar fashion, what remains is the impulse on this opposite extreme to posit gamers chiefly in a celebratory light. It is commendable to map the social significance of gaming for gamers beyond the limits of the DDD, focusing more on the situated lives of gamers. However, those scholars who emphasize the complexity of playing video games are nearly always anxious to show a positive posture towards gaming, perhaps revealing that they too are still caught up in a "sanctioned play" paradigm where one must begin on the defensive in order to overcome unrelenting violence and corruption. Taylor, for example, does a great service by bringing to light the counter-narratives to visualizations of violence against women and by highlighting in depth one video game in particular designed to assist in the process of healing for victims of domestic abuse (Taylor 2011).[29] Her example, called *Wordslinger*, is a web-based game of relatively low graphical fidelity but one that enables the player to experience an affective dimension to roleplaying situations leading up to moments of sexual violence. The player is confronted with familiar abusive male protagonists but is also afforded the opportunity to change the narrative or to speak out (in the game world) in ways that otherwise might not have been possible during countervailing lived experiences. *Wordslinger*, as an online web game, was also attached to a secured web forum where other players could further discuss and share their experiences, both of the game and of their ongoing problematic relationships. The impulse to celebrate this example as a positive encounter, as well as a moment to reclaim greater agency not only for gamers but for survivors of domestic abuse, is indeed tempting. Women who are also gamers are arguably empowered by gaming in this case, owing to the strengths of the online community.

We see other examples boosting positivity in gaming. Elsewhere, Delamere strives to show virtual worlds and video games in a positive light. Though it has been challenged whether the denizens of *Second Life* ought to qualify as gamers or even whether they may self-identify as such,[30] we see in this now historical example how people with physical disabilities, in some cases highly debilitating, can enjoy and engage in virtual movement not possible under other conditions. "Second Lifers" (perhaps we may call them gamers) find not only a "techno-sociality" towards personal fulfilment but also highly sophisticated action involving a community of others. In several recorded cases, Delamere finds Second Life inhabitants gain significant "social capital" and later deploy those skills and resources, even in one case as a reference to secure gainful employment outside of the virtual world.[31]

It is the shift in argument, however, towards claims about gamers and gaming at large that have become more problematic and present a challenge to overcoming the DDD. *Wordslinger* may constitute an exemplary case towards healing and social justice for women, but the assertion that game scholars should take note and build a consideration of this fringe case further into their own analyses of gamers seems less defensible. One solitary video game that may have helped survivors of domestic abuse says very little about a culture of gaming and less still about a whole series, and indeed a genre, of video games that continues to highlight and promote the crime of violence against women, even in some cases explicitly featuring rape as a core mechanic, for example in the game *Rapeplay* (2006). Other similar games encourage groping high school girls for points, as in *Gal Gun* (2016), or offer gamers questionable freedoms to enact violent encounters with sex workers and other virtual non-player characters, as in the now-infamous open-world games from the franchises of *Grand Theft Auto* (2016) and *Saints Row* (2016). My aim here is not to develop further critiques of these games—literature to that end already abounds—yet it is important that we balance what has been an overwhelming negative view with those case studies that may expand upon our viewpoint.[32]

On the whole, we can trace a trend in game studies that emphasizes gamer sociality for its measured potential to achieve "social good". Scholars deem gaming to be significant because gamers might occasionally be praised for their propensity towards positive transformation within their respective communities using their virtual worlds and platforms for social change. While this is a clear trend in game studies, we see evidence that a balanced approach is prudent when shifting from a lens of disaffection to engagement. Again, one could argue that an optimistic tone is required to leverage a response to the overly critical and demonizing tradition of the DDD. Video games, in the main, are arguably still viewed as played by gamers who become violent, disillusioned, and disengaged.[33] Nevertheless, what much of the positive counter-literature

26 A Politics of Being Gamers

on gaming in effect alerts us to is how practices of play have permeated the social, cultural, and economic lives of gamers, indicating how they are not necessarily technologically overdetermined nor, on the opposite extreme, virtually emancipated from the media powers that permeate their everyday lives.

The Internet and Democracy: Young Citizens

I propose an exploration of gamers as citizens to broaden a portrait of everyday life in gaming communities. However, the framework of citizenship, while productive, is not without its pitfalls and limitations. Principally, our challenge lies in how gamers are more likely to be viewed as citizens-in-waiting. Gamers are perceived as young and not yet fully formed, which presents a first obstacle to overcome.

CLOSE-UP 2: "THE FIGURE OF..."

We cannot formulate complex ideas, let alone critique them, without the use of concepts. Concepts are not only organizing principles, but they also emplace a person (a subject) into any given personal experience. Eventually, concepts grow so embedded in groups of people—sometimes entire societies—that they come to "stand in" for how we think about individual categories of people. This is what we mean by "the figure of ...". There can be many figures, and they are often competing for dominance in thought. For example, the figure of the citizen, the figure of the gamer, or the figure of a politician. These figures can also be written in their shortened form as, for example, the citizen, the gamer, and the politician. Philosophers often use upper-case letters to signify that they are working with conceptual figures and not individual case examples.

The figure of the citizen is presently under heavy strain. There are two developing political narratives in the contemporary West, and in particular within the Anglo-American context, about the direction democratic politics is taking in a "post-Brexit" and a "post-President Trump" time. One direction is to focus on a new "globalism" in which, among other issues, the primary political cause is to defend the rights of migrants and to promote the dissolution of national borders, which function to interrupt the free flow of people and the free trade of goods.[34] A global refugee crisis, now pronounced as never before, requires consideration, as do the imperilled and conflict-ridden networks of international trade (chiefly seen in energy products and consumer goods). The second direction, almost on the opposite extreme yet inextricably linked, gives rise to a renewed sense of nationalism—sometimes labelled as "populism"—that opposes globalist values by rallying around calls for patriotism and a return to the imagined idealism of a strong nation state.[35] This latter trend is insistently racial, extolling the virtues of whiteness and European and/or Anglo-American culture.[36] Amidst tension on both sides, however, there remains a third and much older worry about a perceived decline in civic engagement and a mass resignation from formal politics altogether. This position—also commonly referred to as the democratic deficit—offers a counter-narrative grounded in an information society.[37] From this perspective, people living with the internet and digital technology are less inclined to align themselves politically, unlikely to vote, join political parties, or campaign for social causes, and reluctant to trust the political process, which they perceive to be contaminated by corruption stemming from the economic elite and their private interests.[38] A prevailing question in the face of each of these movements, now perhaps dominated by resignation and resentment, is to ask what transforming role technology plays in shaping ideology and promoting or stifling civic action.[39] Amidst tensions on all sides, the figure of a citizen as a paragon, strong, and standing up for rights and responsibilities to the nation-state is failing.

What is more, young people have been at the centre of concern for the internet and democracy, and this is certainly nothing new looking back on recent history.[40] Shakuntala Banaji and David Buckingham develop an empirical look at what young users in the European Union say and how they use their "new media". They consider whether there is truly such cause for alarm about young people's civic engagement. They delve further into what fundamentally counts as "civic engagement" both online and offline, finding that participation cannot be limited to the use of traditional political websites as the issues represented on such sites now come to form a continuity extending elsewhere on social platforms and encompassing several entirely new concerns for a digital generation.[41] Drawing from a large collection of European Union Studies on a total of 570 "civic websites", including both governmental and non-governmental organizations, they find that young people actually have notable contributions to make. For example, they can and do register as members on international networks, national government sites, NGO forums, and charity organizations, just as they partake in political conversation on issues pertinent to those interest groups as they "tweet", "post", and "comment" on their

28 A Politics of Being Gamers

favoured platforms.[42] They also, I would add, engage in a wide variety of activism—Black Lives Matter, World Pride, Women's Marches—yet it is only a relatively small group of the young citizenry who prefer engaging with traditional institutions and through formal channels, for example, political campaigns and single-issue organizations networks.[43] Instead, those young internet users who do find the time to participate do so overwhelmingly online and on their own terms, harbouring concurrently some level of resentment and alienation rather than empowerment as subjects of and to the nation state.[44] Furthermore, as revealed through focus groups to accompany an analysis of "big data", young people are visibly critical of traditional political platforms yet by no means consider themselves apathetic.[45] They report that it is not something inherent to technology and/or the internet that perpetuates the rifts they experience; that is to say, they do not go online to disengage. To the contrary, they feel more engaged online and claim to do so *politically,* despite their discussions being out of alignment with the pedagogy of governments and institutions.[46]

"'Civic Play" and "Learner Citizens"

Still, the figure of the citizen remains in question, if only to ponder what the future holds for politics in this digital age. To bridge this perceived gap between the democratic deficit and an alleged diminished civic capability for a young digital generation, there are those who continue to position young citizens as an issue for civics education. Manifest initiatives in this direction are designed to capture youth interest in technology and leverage the internet to ensure the continuance of the democratic process for future prosperity. W. Lance Bennet, Chris Wells, and Allison Rank (2008), for example, view this as a necessary change in paradigms towards citizenship in a digital age. Their answer to the perennial question of how civics education can keep pace with the changing political identifications and practices of new generations is to acknowledge different modes of citizenship and to respect the learning styles of the young that are increasingly interactive, networked, participatory, and heavily mediated: "Most school-based approaches reflect traditional paradigms of dutiful citizenship (DC) oriented to government through parties and voting, with citizens forming attentive publics who follow events in the news. While this model may appeal to some young people, research suggests that it produces mixed learning outcomes, and may not capture the full range of learning and engagement styles of recent generations of citizens, self-actualized citizens (AC)".[47]

The apparent problem here is one of old educational and social values reinforcing the "Dutiful Citizen"—a citizen who votes and engages as well as learns from political parties—that can often stand in opposition to the "Actualized Citizen", a person embodying political identities and enacting technological practices that form alternative civic orientations, one who also seeks to be a part of a "critical" rather than "incumbent" democracy.[48] We ought to be careful to indicate how to deploy these terms not only with reference to ideal types. The figure of a dutiful citizen, or alternatively, an actualized citizen, does not apply, for instance, to all members of a generational group, as there are well-documented circumstances where a radically different style of politics has surfaced among the young, who exhibit a sense of obligation to follow traditional print media or to vote along party lines. There are, as well, observable cases in the elderly who embrace more fluid styles and reject the overwhelmingly conservative viewpoints of their peers, absconding—for instance, as they did in the liberation movements of the 1950s and 1960s—from their responsibilities to participate in government-centred activities and institutions in favour of a radically new body politic. The consensus, however, is that there is a pattern revealed in survey research that warns of a marked generational departure from dutiful civic practices in younger generations—young people tend to favour more personally expressive or self-actualizing affiliations—and this is a critical concern as it appears that only a small minority are taking up their rights and responsibilities to get involved in issues of national and international interest.

Importantly, there are variances in degree between different figures of the citizen, yet with each conceptual effort, we maintain the goal of rethinking civic learning and not suggesting only one correct model of citizenship. The educational intent is not necessarily to elevate alternative forms of citizenship in the young as Actualized Citizens to the level of acceptability of Dutiful Citizens; rather, it is to leverage behaviours and interests and to inculcate new political agendas into the main political structures. Indeed, young people are perhaps more sympathetic towards peer-to-peer communication, preferring direct action in place of representative democracy, and mistrusting traditional political organizations and groups.[49] In all, the goal is to find a productive convergence of citizenship models, a healthy bridge between what has historically been called the "Managed Citizen" and the "Autonomous Citizen".[50] This is to say that young citizens ought to be taught how to navigate established conventions such as campaigning for democratic parties, voting on their representation, and digesting major journalism outlets whilst also learning to keep a critical mind and to embrace activism in cases of staunch disagreements against the status quo.

30 A Politics of Being Gamers

New imperatives arrive with the mandate of bolstering a civics curriculum. Especially in a North American context, this has been about the development of new tools and virtual environments for young citizenship education.[51] The rationale for developing educational programs for promoting youth civic engagement in the United States is supported for similar reasons as they are in the contexts already established in other areas—namely, to strengthen identities in young citizens who spend increasingly longer periods of time online and who seem disillusioned with their political representation and the political process in general. What is relatively less common in the UK, EU, and Australian contexts is an American turn towards video games to promote learning.[52] American higher education institutions have a long tradition of research and development in the field of "serious games".[53] In this regard, instructional designer Robert L. Appelman is notable for designing a framework intended to facilitate the knowledge gap between educators and game designers—the former who may wish to leverage games to better achieve their learner aims, and the latter being well-established commercial video game designers of captivating interactive experiences.[54] Responding to early work in "serious games", there has in recent years been reciprocal interest from outside of the academy, with the most prominent annual commercial Games Developer Conference (GDC) now hosting a regular Educational Summit to allow for cross pollination and sharing of complimentary design language between industries.[55]

For Marina Umaschi Bers, author of *Let the Games Begin: Civic Playing on High-Tech Consoles* (2010), the potential impact of video games on civic learning has already been made clear.[56] The potential to promote social and civic engagement through game play has in fact existed for several years and has even been well documented by game scholars in such titles as *Civilization* and *Sim City*, in which Squire and Barab (2004) argue that there is an observable educational benefit for gamers to learn about historical contexts and to broaden their understanding of the political decision-making process.[57] To this, one can add authoring kits in which developers enable young people to produce their own video games and develop conceptually rich projects that simulate the challenges of community decision-making.[58] Finally, there are games that offer young people "participatory cultures", thereby serving as a soft entry into civic engagement.[59] Other more direct video game interventions also encourage and engage political questions and skillsets—for example, *On the Campaign Trail*, developed at Kent State University, in which players simulate U.S. Senate election campaigns; *Democracy* and *Democracy 2*, which are simulation games developed by Positech Games to take on the responsibilities and decisions of a president or prime minister of a democratic government dealing with tax, foreign policy, and/or transportation; and, finally, *Superpower*, a web-based video game centered on role-playing governments from real-world nations.[60] Some will argue that "Civic Play" is a source of untapped potential for educators and instructional designers, but more to the point, it embodies a healthy intersection between gaming and formal civic participation.

Though there is evidence of what one might label civic attitudes being exhibited as gamers reflect and make informed judgements about issues in their video games, there is reason for caution against drawing causal links from video games to actual traditional civic behaviours such as voting, community service, activism, petitioning, and joining grass-roots organizations. Bers herself is absolute on this, stating that "No popular video games yet tap into the potential of linking game playing with real-life civic behaviours and community participation".[61] However, there is small evidence, if one digs long enough, for example, a sole quantitative study conducted on the Pew Internet and American Life Project, which found that 44 per cent of youth play "civic games", and concluded definitively that of this group, a majority also go on to enact similar knowledge and skills in an offline context.[62]

Part of the problem remains that young people on the internet are overwhelmingly conceptualized as "Learner Citizens," whose contributions, if they are to occur at all, are allegedly ill-informed and thus not to be taken seriously. Paradoxically, this is a sentiment that comes alongside a lasting rhetoric that young people simply need to participate more regardless of the quality or content of their positions, which is to say they must vote and contribute new ideas as well as articulate their own interests, and that these are inherently good things for an incumbent democracy. Young people should become a greater part of the civic conversation, take civic action, and dedicate themselves more dutifully to their communities offline. Pertinent to this book, there have also been notable attempts to conflate younger citizens as necessarily also "being digital" and enthralled by their technology, always online and playing video games. The educational focus on the internet and video games is one that presumes in the first place that technology is the problem, yet also that it can often be the solution—that something about this medium and the styles of communication it supports do not count as desirable forms of participation but could one day be co-opted and refashioned into a positive civic force in the political sphere.[63]

Perhaps it is best to distinguish between the Dutiful Citizen and the Actualized Citizen. When extended to a discussion of video games and gaming, however, such efforts show that gamers are considered to be

32 A Politics of Being Gamers

insufficiently engaged, despite the likelihood of their being self-actualized and very much connected within their everyday virtual worlds. Civic Play is therefore designated as a means by which to bring gamers into line with their duty, to co-opt video games as a form of political training for a group that we may presume to be disenfranchised and closed off.

ACTIVITY 2

Civic Play is explored critically in this chapter, but that is not to say it is an activity that ought to be completely replaced or ignored. How could you use the idea of Civic Play to explore identities and responsibilities? Furthermore, what happens when we think about video games as tools to shape and empower Dutiful Citizens. Is this essential to repairing a fractured democracy?

Going Around in "Magic Circles"

If gamers are not to be seen as social and political recluses or incomplete citizens, what is it that keeps them from being considered "good citizens"? Another part of the answer lies in key debates over a question often at the core of most video game scholarship: *What is a video game?*

For the most part, spatiality has served as the defining element in video game theory. This starting foundation has dominated the literature as scholars have built upon a canon of theory anchoring the meaning of play on experiences in/of virtual worlds. While this may seem contrary to the more recent literature discussed at the start of this chapter, regarding new trends from sociology and anthropology towards the study of gamers in situated contexts, such incongruences are resolved by the following foundational premise: One ought always to interpret games on their own terms and on their respective "turf", only thereafter moving onwards to building an understanding of the broader social and cultural import of gaming. Gamers should be evaluated based on their activity and their relationships to the spaces that set the scene for video games.

Despite widespread advocacy for a spatial approach—that is, the study of the video game as a particular kind of space—the notion of the virtual world as a distinct space and one that sets up boarders and divisions may trigger anxieties and mistrust for some, especially in view of spatiality as a theorization that is often suspected of reproducing false dichotomies or possibly even spreading an insidious binary thinking that confuses what is "real" and "unreal". Such anxiety is born of older divisions in the case of early game studies, where theoretical spatial splits surface in the work of the ludologists. These theorists support their claims by building upon the notion that video games constitute play spaces (both figurative and literal grounds) that exist outside the boundaries of normal life; within their core design, games imply a conscious step into realms that are separated from an often cruel and unforgiving real world.

Classic game theorists Huzinga (1955) and later Caillois (1958) considered similar "non-serious" and exclusive spaces to be actual suppressions of both time and space in which zones exist for pure ludic enjoyment.[64] For Huizinga, this meant that, among other qualities, all games could offer "magic circles", in which new rules apply both for play and also of/for being "homo-ludens". Salen and Zimmerman (2004) later summarized this particular "ethos of play" best for video games by outlining the "magic circle", emphasizing its peculiar and seemingly paradoxical nature:

> Although the magic circle is merely one of the examples in Huizinga's list of 'play-grounds,' the term is used here as shorthand for the idea of a special place in time and space created by a game. The fact that the magic circle is just that—a circle—is an important feature of this concept. As a closed circle, the space it circumscribes is enclosed and separate from the real world. As a marker of time, the magic circle is like a clock: it simultaneously represents a path with a beginning and end, but one without beginning and end. The magic circle inscribes a space that is repeatable, a space both limited and limitless. In short, a finite space with infinite possibility.[65]

It is precisely this proclaimed space of limitless possibility that both excites game scholars and leaves room for scepticism about the circle's true hold on the mediated processes that transpire in virtual worlds. Falcao and Ribeiro (2011), for example, when theorizing "the whereabouts of play" resist the temptation to simply inherit an understanding of the dynamics of video game play as something essential to isolated magic circles.[66] Without overriding the circle logic entirely, they maintain their enthusiasm for the video game space by opting to reveal its power in connection with players as subject agents. Gamers, they argue, are not simply encircled by a limited environment inside video games; rather, they are specially equipped *to transform* their virtuality by inhabiting the space of magic circles and transforming their social identities at the same time. This is a process of social construction that is achieved through player dialogue and unique player activity. Gaming, therefore, is full of "fluid forms" which augment the magic circle as well as the material world in which it was created, and

34 A Politics of Being Gamers

this is because both are co-constituted: "Our proposal, then, is that the magic circle does not separate effectively the game world from reality, rather it acts as a mediation tool assisting the player in how they deal with the different sides of the universe—and not with *two universes*".[67] This important theoretical move is supported by a shift in the technology of video games and the culture of play, as it has been the general trend over the past several decades for gamers to migrate online and to make use of new tools and abilities in massively multiplayer online games, streaming as well, fostering all new subject agency and opening up the universe for communities to connect across differences.

Anxiety may persist as simply calling the magic circle another side of the universe rather than two universes, and claiming that all sides are essentially one shape, does not necessarily erase the privilege of one facet over another; thus, we risk emphasizing, in the end, a return to the age-old spatial divide. While the history of video game studies now appears to have arrived at a moment of greater clarity in dealing with the medium, formerly studied as "object games" in isolation and now gradually becoming better understood as integrated into a gaming culture where gamers play together on a massive scale, the meaning of a video game is always part of a complex amalgam that is resistant to generalized categorization. Moreover, it is particularly problematic even to suggest that any size group of games is fundamentally similar, since such theoretical and categorical thinking all too often detracts from important questions regarding how games are used by gamers individually and collectively in situated contexts.[68] Nevertheless, for the sake of shorthand, it may be helpful to theorize the three—video games, gamers, and gaming—as distinct forms, that is, to insist upon their categories in order to stake claims and articulate findings in research. The most fruitful analytical platform, then, is one that strives to acknowledge a clear focus on video games, albeit as multifaceted, while simultaneously observing the intersections between gamers who play in a variety of ways and who also form communities of play on streaming platforms such as Twitch. This is not to abandon the spatial logic of the video game as a discrete space but rather to grant the complexities of a gaming space and its relation to gamers as important subjects.

Given that more people around the globe are settling in and getting comfortable inhabiting worlds online, there is indeed as much to shock and disturb as there is to innovate and create.[69] However, as Judy Wajcman suggests, it is time to get past "speculative hyperbole" to see that "society is more than its technology, but also that technology is more than its equipment".[70] Pertinent to this, we build onwards from such a theoretical claim, namely that a sustained fascination with the inner workings of a technology (magic circles) will not get us any closer to an understanding of its social significance. We may define this present digital age as a time when people are increasingly unable to comprehend a socio-material existence that is entirely separate from gadgets and the internet, and increasingly so from their video games. Importantly, this is not to say that any given technology determines social existence or, on the contrary, that this is an age of our total mastery over machines[71]. Binary oppositions no longer figure into the logic. Instead, computers, the internet, and video games, among other advances in the software that they run, give cause for hope, just as technologies have in decades past, while also simultaneously warranting a more critical perspective. In any case, it is not only unproductive but now also counter-intuitive to search for rigid distinctions between the "real" and the "virtual", since networked innovations call for careful investigation tailored to the unique contexts on the ground as these simultaneously extend into virtual space. Ultimately, preoccupations with simplistic questions like, "What is a video game?" impede any serious thinking about gamers as citizens of any importance.

Conclusion: Conceptualizing Gamer Citizens

Moral panics towards video games and gamers have somewhat dissipated in recent years, but their lasting effects continue to haunt intellectual thinking. Video games are part of a massive consumer media industry that began in the late 19th century, and they have passed through many phases of development since their early beginnings as "electronic amusements" 60 years ago. During that time, scholarly interest has coalesced around two research standpoints. First, there have been those who are interested in media form and content, which is to say, the media effects of video game play on individuals and groups of gamers. Such investigations are rooted in the "behaviorist tradition"—for example, building on Albert Bandura's "social learning theory", variations of "catharsis theory", general arousal theory, and cognitive models of aggression.[72]

A second group, which has been critically engaged with the first standpoint, comprises studies on the ethnographic, semiotic, and cultural significance of gameplay and the social engagement between gamers and their "virtual worlds" focusing on human agency, creativity, and subjectivity. The research contained within this camp (one might call it a camp of social research) has tended to focus on gender representation in video game communities, challenging, for example, the success and/or failures in establishing positive "genderspaces" within gaming culture while also pursuing a few ethical and political critiques of racialized gameplay and design practices.[73] While debates on all sides have taken on a decidedly softer, more "peaceful" tone in recent years, studies of gamers of all walks of life continue to drive a literature that sustains interest and notably also generates stern critique from a variety of disciplines, each contributing in changing ways to the perceived limits of acceptability and accountability within a complex of activity surrounding video games.[74]

Gamer or citizen? This is a question that yet begs answering. It is a question that not only emerges when following the recent examples of gamers who have interfaced politically and publicly, as we saw reported in the press at the start of this chapter, but one that also arises when engaging with video game studies, digital citizenship studies, and alternative internet studies collectively. This chapter presents a canvas from which to show how gamers can be considered in a more serious, inclusive and, indeed, more political light, but it is my intention to show that we ought to name these considerations properly. We should name these factors as part of a larger question of/for citizenship in a digital age. This chapter finds that a gamer figure who is responsible, upstanding, and politically active—a "Gamer Citizen"—remains largely unimaginable, and by consequence, such a figure has remained out of conceptual reach. The move towards an exploration of gaming as centered on gamers, while a welcome development, has not come far enough to shift the terms of discussion towards a question of how we might regard gamers as active subjects and come to understand their sociality for its wider political implications. To engage the chapters that follow, there is a need to acknowledge the actualities of a gamer's interconnected life, as studies have recently begun to reveal, yet to do so in a fashion that examines how power and resistance both operate within this dynamic to produce a figure that shapes alternative political subjects. Importantly, this is not only a question of a virtual life versus a material life but also of a political life in the everyday for gamers.

Gamers should strive towards the Dutiful Citizen, absolutely, just as they may yet prove to align well with the Actualized Citizen, but gamers must also shape a new figure of politics, the "Gamer Citizen", whom I propose is characterized by being: (1) not a learner, but rather an expert; (2) not primarily disaffected, instead highly engaged and capable of sophisticated action as well as strong leadership; and (3) possessing mastery and skill over the building of communities both online and offline. The Gamer Citizen does not need to be antithetical to any other formulation of citizen subject. There is room in the theoretical landscape alongside other figures, but it will be our responsibility to show when and how real citizens may co-exist and collide. The data and narrative scripts that I present in subsequent chapters of this book are ethnographic in nature.

It is, finally, my contention that if we are to explore any working concept of gamers as citizens, we must find that theoretical footing through a respectful and deep examination of their everyday lives and experiences.

QUESTIONS

1. What is the Dominant Discourse of Disaffection (DDD)?
2. Who might practically fit the figure of a "Learner Citizen"? What about the Dutiful or Actualized Citizen? Do you know of any people who fit these concepts?
3. Is there a "Magic Circle" of gaming? If so, what is its primary function?
4. How might you conceptualize the Gamer Citizen differently?

Notes

1 BBC. "Alexandria Ocasio-Cortez Among Us game watched by 400,000," *bbc.com*. https://www.bbc.com/news/technology-54630330 (accessed September 17, 2023). Pokimane [@Pokimane], *Twitch*. https://www.twitch.tv/pokimane/about (accessed September 17, 2023); HasanAbi [@HasanAbi], *Twitch*. https://www.twitch.tv/hasanabi (accessed September 17, 2023).
2 Twitch (2020). "Don't Lurk on Democracy! Play your part and inspire your community to vote on November 3rd." Nov 1, 2020. URL: https://blog.twitch.tv/en/2020/11/01/install-votebot2020-today-and-help-get-out-the-vote/
3 The Kappa emoji has been used over one billion times on Twitch since its release in 2011. See: "StreamElements Chat Stats". https://stats.streamelements.com/ (accessed September 17, 2023). The average demographic of a user on Twitch is male and twenty-one years of age. Ruby, D. (2023). "Twitch Statistics 2023 — (Users, Revenue & Insights)." *DemandSage*.
4 Taylor T.L. (2006) Play Between Worlds: Exploring Online Game Culture. The MIT Press
5 Hernandez, P. (2019). "On Twitch, talking about politics can be taboo." *Polygon*. https://www.polygon.com/2019/8/30/20835568/twitch-politics-streaming-mixer-trump-shootings (accessed September 17, 2023).
6 Twitch has proven to be a platform ripe for the spread of racism, for the perpetuation of anti-'LGBTQ' comments, and for the amplification of hate speech. There have been several high-profile controversies as well attempts to respond to this scourge of the platform. See for example: Grayson, N. (2016). "Twitch Chat Racism Changed Hearthstone Pro Terrence Miller's Career." Kotaku. https://kotaku.com/hearthstone-pro-terrence-miller-hopes-to-clean-up-twitc-1787551043 (accessed September 17, 2023); Plunkett, L. (2023). "Call of Duty Pulls Twitch Streamer Nickmercs' Skin Over Anti-LGBTQ

38 A Politics of Being Gamers

Comment." Kotaku. https://www.yahoo.com/lifestyle/call-duty-pulls-youtube-streamer-023000443.html (accessed September 17, 2023); and Browning, K. (2020). "Twitch Cracks Down on Hate Speech and Harassment." The New York Times. https://www.nytimes.com/2020/12/09/technology/twitch-harassment-policy.html (accessed September 17, 2023).

7 Stephen, B. (2019). "The Old Man And The Stream: The campaign wants everyone it can find on board, and is working with Streamlabs on Twitch to do it." *The Verge*. https://www.theverge.com/2019/8/15/20804614/bernie-sanders-twitch-presidential-campaign-gamers-streaming-donations-streamlabs-fec (accessed September 17, 2023).

8 Davies, H. (2020). "Spatial Politics at Play: Hong Kong Protests and Videogame Activism." Digital Games Research Association DiGRA Australia 2020.

9 Fain, C. (2021). "13 LGBTQ+ Twitch Streamers You Should Be Following." GameRant. https://gamerant.com/lgbtq-twitch-streamers-to-follow/

10 Seavon, F. (2022). "'Gaymers' Are Taking Brazil by Storm." Wired.com. https://www.wired.com/story/brazilian-twitch-streamers-drag/

11 Zwiezen, Z. (2022). "Epic & Fortnite Players Raise $36 Million For Ukraine In Just 24 Hours." Kotaku. https://kotaku.com/fortnite-epic-ukraine-35-million-donations-charity-russ-1848683029

12 Grossman, D., & DeGaetano, G. (2014, first 1999). Stop teaching our kids to kill: A call to action against TV, movie & video violence. New York: Crown.

13 Grossman, "Stop Teaching our Kids to Kill," 9.

14 It is alarming that Grossman and DeGaetano introduce their book with the section title 'It's Not Normal.' Only 86 words were changed between the original 1999 publication and the most recent 2014 edition indicating that gaming today is still "not normal" and gaming is particularly dangerous.

15 Harris, R.J. (2014). A Cognitive Psychology of Mass Communication. Lawrence Erlbaum Associates, Publishers Mahwah, New Jersey. 29.

16 Hall, S. (1995). Modernity: An introduction to modern societies. Cambridge: Polity Press. 5.

17 Kroker offers a reader in "critical digital studies" that is particularly attuned to how learning to "decode" the digital reveals traumas and other symptoms of the social which are co-dependent on factors both material and technical (Kroker 2013). See: Kroker, A. & Marilousie Kroker (2013). Critical Digital Studies: A Reader, Second Edition. Toronto: University of Toronto Press. Others as well under the umbrella of a whole emerging discipline called "the digital humanities" acknowledge significant benefits to thinking through technological platforms, indeed to thinking with technology, both to investigate its invaluable uses as constructive tool and to acknowledge still a "darker side" of human machine relations (O'Sullivan 2022, Chun & Rhody 2014). See: O'Sullivan, J (2022). The Bloomsbury Handbook to the Digital Humanities. New York: Bloomsbury Handbooks, and Chun. W. & Lisa Marie Rhody (2014). Working the Digital Humanities: Uncovering Shadows between the Dark and the Light. differences: A Journal of Feminist Cultural Studies. (2014) 25 (1): 1–25.

18 See: Crawford, G (2012). Video Gamers. London: Routledge; Taylor T.L. (2006) Play Between Worlds: Exploring Online Game Culture. The MIT Press; and Walz, S.P. (2010). Toward a Ludic Architecture: The Space of Play and Games: ETC Press

19 Crawford G., Victoria K. Gosling and Ben Light (2011). Online Gaming in Context: The Social and Cultural Significance of Online Games. Routledge

20 Castronova, E. (2008). Synthetic worlds: The business and culture of online games. University of Chicago press. 47.

A Politics of Being Gamers **39**

21 Park and Hee Lee discuss how real-money transactions, often prevalent in massively multiplayer online games, build upon an interplay between gamer community and video games with less fixed narrative scripts for players to follow. Such games and the gamers who play them are more open to trade and engage profit generating motives (Park and Hee Lee, 2017). See: Park, B & Duk Hee Lee (2017). "The Interplay between Real Money Trade and Narrative Structure in Massively Multiplayer Online Role-Playing Games" in International Journal of Computer Games Technology. Volume 2017

22 Dyer-Witheford has captured the rising class and economic inequality best for gaming and a digital age warning of the rise of a "cybernetic proletariat." See: Dyer-Witheford, N. (2015). Cyber Proletariat: Global Labour in the Digital Vortex. Pluto Press.

23 McGonigal, J. (2011). Reality is broken: Why games make us better and how they can change the world. Penguin. 13

24 Poole, S. (2000). Trigger happy: Videogames and the entertainment revolution. Skyhorse Publishing Inc.

25 Thornham, H. (2011). Ethnographies of the Videogame: Gender, narrative and praxis. Farnham, Surrey, England: Ashgate.

26 Thornham, H. (2011). Ethnographies of the Videogame.

27 A number of scholars in the 1990s explored the explicit violence in video games and its media effects on gamers, but a few as well developed the further argument that these behaviours tend to spread along gender lines, that is boys and men are more susceptible to the corrupting influence of video games. Taking a different approach and seeking to celebrate video games, Jenkins notes that gendered game design and player practices function to exclude girls relegating most to "pink ghettos" and prohibiting more from experiencing for themselves the wonders of virtual worlds (Jenkins 1998). See: Jenkins, H (1998). From Barbie to Mortal Kombat: Gender and Computer Games. Cambridge, MA: The MIT Press.

28 Crawford, "Video Gamers," See Chapter 1.

29 Taylor, K. E. (2011) "Wordslinger: visualizing physical abuse in a virtual environment"; in Crawford G., Victoria K. Gosling and Ben Light (2011). Online Gaming in Context: The Social and Cultural Significance of Online Games. Routledge. 266–278.

30 Boellstorff, T. (2008). Coming of age in Second Life: An anthropologist explores the virtually human. Princeton University Press.

31 Delamere, F. M. (2011). "Second Life as a Digitally Mediated Third Place: Social Capital in Virtual World Communities;" in Crawford G., Victoria K. Gosling and Ben Light (2011). Online Gaming in Context: The Social and Cultural Significance of Online Games. Routledge. 242

32 See: Kutner, L. Cheryl Olson (2008). Grand Theft Childhood: The Surprising Truth About Violent Video Games and What Parents Can Do. Simon & Schuster: New York; DeVane, B. Kurt D. Squire (2008). "The Meaning of Race and Violence in Grand Theft Auto." in Games and Culture Vol 3, Issue 3–4, pp. 264–285; and Hollingdale, J. & Tobias Greitemeyer (2013). "The Changing Face of Aggression: The Effect of Personalized Avatars in a Violent Video Game on Levels of Aggressive Behavior." in Journal of Applied Social Psychology. Vol 43–9. 1862–1868.

33 See: Anderson, C.A., & Bushman. B.J. (2001) "Effects of violent video games on aggressive behavior, aggressive cognition, aggressive affect, physiological arousal, and prosocial behavior: A meta-analytical review of the scientific literature." Psychological Science, 12, 353–359; and Lee, Kwan Min; Peng, Wei

40 A Politics of Being Gamers

(2009), "What Do We Know About Social and Psychological Effects of Computer Games? A Comprehensive Review of the Current Literature" in Playing Video Games: Motives, Responses, and Consequences, Vorderer, Peter and Jennings Bryant (eds): Taylor & Francsis e-Library

34 See: Haidt, Jonathan (2016). "When and why nationalism beats globalism [online]." Policy: A Journal of Public Policy and Ideas, Vol. 32, No. 3, Spring 2016: 46–53. Availability: <http://search.informit.com.au/documentSummary; dn=405917723085484;res=IELAPA; and Rosenboim, O. (2017). Emergence of globalism: Visions of world order in Britain and the United States, 1939-1950. Princeton: Princeton University Press.

35 Why "populism" is an appropriate ideological standpoint to describe present day politics in a globalized context remains to be seen. The term is gaining traction but may not necessarily indicate anything more than a mass dissatisfaction with established political parties and emerging technocratic interests. This is a backlash repeated many times in history, as Caramani (2017) suggests. Another interpretation surfacing is to label populism as simply a new face for white supremacy as Hage (2012) also indicates. See: Caramani, D. (2017). "Will vs. Reason: The Populist and Technocratic Forms of Political Representation and Their Critique to Party Government." American Political Science Review, 111(1), 54–67, and Hage, G. (2012). White Nation: Fantasies of White Supremacy in a Multicultural Society. Routledge.

36 Miller-Idriss, C. (2009). Blood and culture: Youth, right-wing extremism, and national belonging in contemporary Germany. Durham: Duke Univ. Press.

37 Usage of the term 'democratic deficit' has been pervasive in the literature; suggests Dahl (1994), Crombez (2003), Pharr (2000), Putnam (2002), Moravcsik (2002), Hix (2006), Warren (2009), Norris (2011). See: Dahl, Robert A. (1994) "A Democratic Dilemma: System Effectiveness Versus Citizen Participation", Political Science Quarterly, 109/1; Crombez, C. (2003) "The democratic deficit in the European Union: much ado about nothing?", European Union Politics, 4/1; Pharr, Susan and Robert Putnam. Eds. 2000. Disaffected Democracies: What's Troubling the Trilateral Countries? Princeton, NJ: Princeton University Press; Putnam, Robert D. Ed. 2002 Democracies in Flux. Oxford: Oxford University Press; Moravcsik, Andrew (2002) "In Defense of the 'Democratic Deficit': Reassessing the Legitimacy of the European Union". Journal of Common Market Studies, 40(4): 603–34; Hix, Simon and Andreas Follesdal (2006) "Why There is a Democratic Deficit in the EU: A Response to Majone and Moravcsik", Journal of Common Market Studies, 44(3); Warren, Mark E. (2009), "Citizen Participation and Democratic Deficits: Considerations from the Perspective of Democratic Theory," in Activating the Citizen: Dilemmas of Participation in Europe and Canada, eds. Joan DeBardeleben and Jon Pammett, pp. 17–40; Norris, Pippa. (2011). Democratic Deficits. New York, NY: Oxford University Press.

38 Cooke, Nicole A. (2017), "Posttruth, Truthiness, and Alternative Facts: Information Behavior and Critical Information Consumption for a New Age," The Library Quarterly 87, no. 3 (July 2017): 211–221.

39 Feenberg, A., & Feenberg, A. (2002). Transforming technology: A critical theory revisited. New York, NY: Oxford University Press.

40 See: Bellamy, Christine & Charles D. Raab (2001). "Electronic Democracy and the 'Mixed Polity': Symbiosis or Conflict?." The Joint Sessions of Workshops of the European Consortium of Political Research, Grenoble, 6-11 April 2001; Bennett, W L (2008). Civic Life Online: Learning How Digital Media Can

Engage Youth. Cambridge, Mass: MIT Press; Bennett, W L. (2009), Chris Wells & Allison Rank. Young Citizens and Civic Learning: Two Paradigms of Citizenship in the Digital Age. Center for Communication & Civic Engagement. URL: http://engagedyouth.org/uploads/2008/08/youngcitizens_clo_finalaug_l.pdf; and Collin, Philippa (2015). Young Citizens and Political Participation in a Digital Society: Addressing the Democratic Disconnect. Palgrave Macmillan.

41 Buckingham, D., Rebekah Willett (2006). Digital Generations: Children, Young People and New Media, Routledge: London.

42 Banaji, Shakuntala, and David Buckingham (2013). The Civic Web: Young People, the Internet and Civic Participation. The MIT Press.

43 Shakuntala, and Buckingham. "The Civic Web: Young People, the Internet and Civic Participation"; and Collin, Philippa (2015). Young Citizens and Political Participation in a Digital Society: Addressing the Democratic Disconnect. Palgrave Macmillan.

44 Shakuntala, and Buckingham. "The Civic Web: Young People, the Internet and Civic Participation." 154.

45 Bennett, Wells & Rank. "Young Citizens and Civic Learning: Two Paradigms of Citizenship in the Digital Age." Ibid.

46 Wells, C. (2013). "Two Eras of Civic Information and the Evolving Relationship Between Civil Society Organizations and Young Citizens" in. New Media & Society. Volume: 16 issue: 4, page(s): 615–636.

47 Bennett. "Civic Life Online: Learning How Digital Media Can Engage Youth." 1.

48 See furthermore: Collin, Philippa (2015). Young Citizens and Political Participation in a Digital Society: Addressing the Democratic Disconnect. Palgrave Macmillan.

49 Bennett. "Civic Life Online: Learning How Digital Media Can Engage Youth." 6.

50 Coleman, Stephen & Jay G. Blumler (2009). The Internet and Democratic Citizenship: Theory, Practice, and Policy. Cambridge University Press

51 Raphael, C., Christine Bachen, Kathleen-M. Lynn, Jessica Baldwin-Philippi, KristenA. McKee (2009). "Games For Civic Learning: A Conceptual Framework and Agenda for Research and Design." in Games and Culture; Vol 5. Issue 2, 199–235.

52 Collin renders several excellent case studies from the contexts of UK, EU, and Australian youth in politics. Their participation, leadership, and management skills are not only notable but sometimes exceptional with self-initiated organizations populated by hundreds of staff members reaching out to millions of young citizens on important issues in a digital age. These include but are not limited to online outreach to people suffering mental health issues, special online education, and training initiatives for people with limited access and environmental cleanup campaigns. See: Collin, Philippa (2015). Young Citizens and Political Participation in a Digital Society: Addressing the Democratic Disconnect. Palgrave Macmillan. It should also be noted that beyond education there is also an intense American commitment to using video games for military training. For a recent revisit of this longstanding tradition and its consequences to a discourse of disaffection for gamers, see Sparrow, R., Rebecca Harrison, Justin Oakley, and Brendan Keogh (2015). "Playing for Fun, Training for War: Can Popular Claims About Recreational Video Gaming and Military Simulations be Reconciled?" in Games and Culture Vol 13, Issue 2. pp. 174–192.

53 Wouters, P., Christof Van Numwegen, Herrer Van Oostendorp, and Erik D. Van Der Spek (2013). "A Meta-Analysis of the Cognitive and Motivational

Effects of Serious Games." in Journal of Educational Psychology: American Psychological Association: DOI: 10.1037/a0031311.

54 See: Appelman, R., & Wilson, J. (2006). "Games and simulations for training: From group activities to virtual reality." In J. Pershing (Ed.), Handbook of human performance technology. San Francisco: Pfeiffer; Appelman, R.L. (2005). "Designing Experiential Modes: A Key Focus for Immersive Learning Environments." TechTrends: 49.3: 64–74; and Appelman, R.L. (2007). "Serious Game Design: Balancing Cognitive and Affective Engagement." In Organizing and Learning through Gaming and Simulation: Proceedings of ISAGA 2007.

55 GDC (2017). Game Developers Conference Call for Submissions - Educators Summit. UBM Technology Group. URL: http://www.gdconf.com/conference/c4p/summits.html.

56 Bers, M. (2010). "Let the Games Begin: Civic Playing on High-Tech Consoles." Review of General Psychology, 14, 147–153.

57 Squire, K., & Barab, S. (2004, June). "Replaying history: Engaging urban underserved students in learning world history through computer simulation games." Paper presented at the Sixth International Conference on Learning Sciences, Santa Monica, CA.

58 Papert, S. (1980). Mindstorms: Children, computers and powerful ideas. New York: Basic Books.

59 Jenkins, H (2006). Fans Bloggers and Gamers. New York (NY): New York University Press.

60 Bers. "Let the Games Begin." 150.

61 Bers. "Let the Games Begin." 151.

62 Lenhart, A., Joseph Kahne, Ellen Middaugh, Alexandra Rankin Macgill, Chris Evans, Jessica Vitak (2008). "Tees, Video Games, and Civics: Teens' gaming experiences are diverse and include significant social interaction and civic engagement." Pew Internet and American Life Project September 16th 2008: MacArthur.

63 Habermas, Jürgen (1989), The Structural Transformation of the Public Sphere: An Inquiry into a Category of Bourgeois Society, Thomas Burger, Cambridge Massachusetts: The MIT Press, p. 30. ISBN 0-262-58108-6. Translation from the original German, published 1962.

64 See: Huizinga, J. (1955). Homo ludens: A study of the play-element in culture. Boston, MA: The Beacon Press, and Caillois, R. (2001 [1958]) Man, Play and Games (Trans. M. Barash), Urbana, University of Illonois.

65 Salen, K. and E. Zimmerman (2004) Rules of Play: Game Design Fundamentals, London, MIT Press. 96.

66 Falcao, T, Jose Carlos Ribeiro (2011). "The Whereabouts of Play, or How the Magic Circle Helps Create Social Identities in Virtual Worlds." in Online Gaming in Context: The Social and Cultural Significance of Online Games. Eds rawford G., Victoria K. Gosling and Ben Light. Routledge.

67 Falcao & Ribeiro. "The Whereabouts of Play." 132.

68 See: Crawford G., Victoria K. Gosling and Ben Light (2011). Online Gaming in Context: The Social and Cultural Significance of Online Games. Routledge; and Crawford, G (2012). Video Gamers. London: Routledge.

69 Bartlett writes in Dark Web how clandestine and highly criminal transactions continue to occur beneath the surface of what is observable online in the mainstream. The Dark Web is a bulk section that remains unsearchable and undocumented to most average users.

70 Wajcman, Judy (2014). Pressed for Time: The Acceleration of Life in Digital Capitalism. Chicago: University of Chicago Press.

71 I, as well, do not assume equal access, nor do I ignore the fact that still many have no interaction with computers at all.

72 For "social learning theory", see: Bandura, A. (1977). Social Learning Theory. Englewood Cliffs: Prentice-Hall; for "catharsis theory", see: Dominick, Joseph R. (1984). "Videogames, Television Violence, and Aggression in Teenagers" in Journal of Communication Vol 34, Issue 2, pp. 136–147; for "cognitive models of aggression" see: Berlyne, D. E. (1971). Aesthetics and psychobiology. New York: Appleton-Century-Crofts; Anderson, C.A., & Bushman. B.J. (2001) "Effects of violent video games on aggressive behavior, aggressive cognition, aggressive affect, physiological arousal, and prosocial behavior: A meta-analytical review of the scientific literature." Psychological Science, 12, 353–359; and Lee, Kwan Min; Peng, Wei (2009), "What Do We Know About Social and Psychological Effects of Computer Games? A Comprehensive Review of the Current Literature" in Playing Video Games: Motives, Responses, and Consequences, Vorderer, Peter and Jennings Bryant (eds): Taylor & Francsis e-Library; and Das, S., Ahona Ghosh, Sriparna Sha (2023). "Chapter 1: A Review of Gaming Effects on Cognitive Load for Smart Healthcare and Its Security" in Using Multimedia Systems, Tools, and Technologies for Smart Healthcare Services Eds. Ahona Ghosh, Sriparna Saha. IGI Global: 1–28.

73 For literature on "Genderspaces" see: Malkowski, J., & Russworm, T. M. (2017). Gaming representation: Race, gender, and sexuality in video games. Indiana University Press; Jenson, J., & de Castell, S. (2008). "Theorizing Gender and Digital Gameplay: Oversights, Accidents and Surprises." In Eludamos Journal for Computer Game Culture: Vol.2.1: pp. 15–25; Ivory, J.D. (2006) "Still a Man's Game: Gender Representation in Online Reviews of Video Games." In Mass Communication & Society, 9(1), pp. 103–114; Pickard, J. (2003, April 16). "Genderplay: Successes and Failures in Character Designs for Videogames." 2005, Accessed: April 25, 2015. URL: http://www.gamegirladvance.com/archives/2003/04/16/genderplay_successes_and_failures_in_character_designs_for_videogames.html#000316; Jenkins, H (1998). From Barbie to Mortal Kombat: Gender and Computer Games. Cambridge, Massachusetts: The MIT Press. For literature on race and gaming, see: Leonard, D. (2003). "Live in your world, play in ours – Race, video games, and consuming the other." Studies in Media & Information Literacy Education, 3(4), November; Michael, M. (2004). "The Color of Mayhem in a Wave of 'Urban' Games." Accessed October 27th 2011. URL: http://www.nytimes.com/learning/teachers/featured_articles/20040813friday.html; and Patterson, C. B. (2020). Open World Empire: Race, Erotics, and the Global Rise of Video Games. NYU Press: New York.

74 Ferguson and Koinji engage in what they call a "cordial debate" in attempts to address a contemporary context of violence in video games for gamers. See: Ferguson, C. J., & Konijn, E. A. (2015). "She said/he said: A peaceful debate on video game violence." Psychology of Popular Media Culture, 4(4), 397–411.

2

ENCOUNTERING GAMER CITIZENS

Introduction

What is it like to encounter gamers online? Arriving on Twitch can be quite overwhelming for the uninitiated. The first thing that visitors are greeted with is a hosted live stream, much the same as a television channel of the past flashed into view on a glowing display set. There is no explicit instruction on how to proceed or much description of the content itself. Visitors are only met with a few home links, including "browse", "Log in", and "sign up". Twitch assumes a significant degree of web literacy, and as such, the home page does not go out of its way to make introductions or to explain features. Visitors are expected to have an established interest in video games and are understood to be capable of propelling themselves further onto the platform on the strength of their existing commitments. I was drawn to explore live streaming by one particular gamer. I followed him on Twitch because he was to cover an upcoming video game that I was interested in playing, yet the activity of streaming appeared foreign to me at that time when compared to playing a video game on my own. In my case, visiting Twitch created a moment of scepticism about whether this new medium would be able to sustain anyone's interest, and indeed, it never became a mainstay of my own personal media consumption. I learned from this that research on Twitch requires a critical open mind, a great degree of both intellectual and practical flexibility, and a willingness to step outside of what is familiar and comfortable.

Part of that flexibility begins with the exploration and observation of new channels. On Saturday, August 8th, 2015, I watched Syed Sumail Hassan become the youngest professional video game player to surpass $1 million

DOI: 10.4324/9781003341079-3

USD in championship winnings. Born on February 13th, 1999, in Karachi, Pakistan, Sumail immigrated as a teenager with his family, including six siblings, his mother, father, and aunt, to Rosemount, Minnesota. Upon arrival there, he decided to join a local gaming league to continue playing his favourite video game, *Dota 2*. While Sumail is an immensely talented and dedicated gamer, this does not necessarily mark him as exceptional amongst his peers. What does set him apart, as I found through my discussions with his fan community and observing his progress, is the fact that despite his young age and the rigors of moving to a new home and country, he could rise so quickly to the top of one of the fastest-growing and most fiercely competitive professional gaming circuits in the world. Against significant odds and accounting for notable costs in computer equipment and time spent practicing, Sumail's dedication and, crucially, his drive to win led to his being recruited into one of the top competitive teams in the world.

Sumail's manager and recruiter, Charlie Yang, believed his uncanny knowledge and skills would lead to great success if only his talents could be refined by the leadership skills and kinship he would gather from his top-tier peers. Along with thousands of adoring fans, I watched as Sumail and his teammates took first place after less than two years on the professional gaming scene. Sumail, at the young age of 16, had become a "poster boy" playing an important symbolic role in competitive electronic sports (Esports). His story reminds us that America is not only a place where celebrities are born but also a land where dreams are realized, even for gamers and even for immigrants from Pakistan.

As I watched Sumail's victory, I was deeply perplexed at what was occurring on stream. Neither a fan of his nor a player of *Dota 2*, I was nevertheless eager to learn more, joined by the thousands of online viewers who had ostensibly gathered on Twitch to support and celebrate the competition. Though I make the case that Sumail is marked as a particular archetype of immigrant success, I raise him chiefly to discuss the contestations and modalities of resistance that surround him. Through his example, we see that gamers can both sustain and interrupt dominant discourses as they perform themselves as active subjects on live streams. To make sense of Sumail and to capture the subtle meanings and "floating signifiers" in operation behind other similar high-profile framings of gamers in Esports, it is helpful to explore Twitch as a complex and multimodal communications interface that features emoticons or emojis most prominently as political nodes in a "circuit of culture."[1] I argue in this chapter that the notion of the Gamer Citizen is emergent, and emojis have proven an important early step in a cultural and political evolution that gives rise to this new conceptual framing.

The first moment of note during the broadcast of Sumail's story was the frequent and very perturbed "NOT AGAIN" response from viewers in the live chat using "DansGame," a popular emoji for registering displeasure.

46 Encountering Gamer Citizens

This reaction was from viewers who had been repeatedly subjected to a propagandistic video recounting Sumail's story of immigrant success in the "land of opportunity." Their use of "DansGame" and other emojis, notably the "Kappa" emoji, were visual interventions that, when taken together, formulated the early actions and voice of the Gamer Citizen (Table 2.1).

TABLE 2.1 Universal Twitch Emojis.

DansGame

Anele

BibleThump

ResidentSleeper

Kappa

The Emoji Code

For linguists and critical media theorists alike, the study of the codes of language is integral to building knowledge of signification. The meanings of messages are intensely debated now that linguists who are interested in emojis struggle to solve the many problems of comprehension in a digital age. For example, Marcel Danesi argues for the structural significance of an "emoji code" indicating that the internet age is bringing about a rise in visual representation and, along with it, a potential evolution in the writing and literacy systems for all humankind—perhaps our first steps as a species into a natural form of universal digital language. Danesi finds, however, that the transition to emoji speech is evolutionary, not revolutionary, as he discovers in his study that the emoji code is more akin to other natural languages that develop and are susceptible to specific experiences, particular communities, and a sensitivity to political as well as cross-cultural pressures.[2] Building on a similar analytical perspective, Marengo et al. see emoji as an artificial code from which users, especially users of mobile phones, extract meaning derived from an original sentiment.[3] Like a tool invented as shorthand to facilitate communication across great distances and in short periods of time, emojis help us to assess personality and emotion, yet they do not always succeed in being correctly interpreted.[4] Linguists in this area are poised to resolve the many ambiguities of speech and to understand emojis as globally **affective** as well as **effective** forms of digital communication.[5]

CLOSE-UP 1: "AFFECT VS. EFFECT"

The words "affect" and "effect" carry subtle differences in meaning. Generally, to affect something means to influence or to make a change to something, whereas an effect (usually a noun) signifies a result or outcome. In cultural studies, "affect" takes on further meaning, often referring to an observable emotion that is sometimes understood as flowing between bodies and groups. The study of effects in social theory means to study results or outcomes. The study of affect implies a more complex look at the role of emotions that intensify, attract, or divide social relations as well as cultural phenomena.

My contribution to an ostensible emoji code as a basic form of communication departs from the prevailing view, where the use of emoji language is understood in terms of a linear form of meaningful communication. While linguists helpfully inform us on how languages function (or malfunction) as culturally sensitive instruments for encoding and decoding information (i.e. language as a tool), we learn from a critical media perspective how language is more fruitfully studied as a flow of representations and cultural practices (i.e. language as a signifying practice). We use language as a system of signs and symbols, and these do appear at first to serve a particular instrumentality. But discourse is more fluid, and it manifests within a "circuit of culture", a regime that only ever exists within what media theorists call a "complex structure in dominance".[6] Emojis are the new objects of this structure, but they are not mere re-presentations or depictions of what came prior. Instead, we ought to consider emojis more appropriately as "floating signifiers" or "sign-vehicles" in which knowledge is constantly being negotiated, transformed, and performed. It is from this theoretical perspective that any semblance of an emoji code will prove useful. Stuart Hall offers us a "circuit of culture" that can be adapted to help us think about emojis as they appear alongside other nodes linked in a networked regime of representation (Figure 2.1). There are several nodes within the circuit, each contributing in changing ways to the meanings and messages that we encode as well as decode in our common communication. "Representation" is the basic symbolic code; "identity" is our model of personhood; "production" is the system that produces narrative scripts; "consumption" is the means by which we assimilate discourse; and "regulation" the power

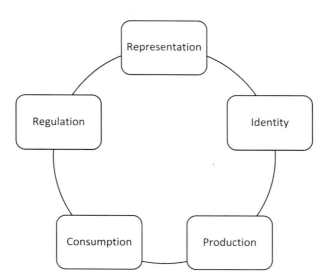

FIGURE 2.1 An adapted representation of Stuart Hall's circuit of culture. Each node in the circuit is adjusted to emphasize how flows intersect in multiple directions.

that enables or constrains certain types of significations. Importantly, no single node in the circuit is necessarily more powerful than any other, and each node contributes to a multidirectional flow that both generates and sustains various branches of culture as well as meaning-making.

Case Study: "The Young Sumail"

In Sumail, we see how gaming economies come to depend on the valorization of professional gamers and the ways this is accomplished on behalf of controlling corporations through the careful crafting of a heroic gamer figure. This is the preferred corporate response to the dominant discourse of disaffection in gaming discussed in Chapter 1, and we see Sumail—or "The Young Sumail" as the Valve Corporation has branded him—as providing a window into an important site of representational and cultural struggle. Sumail is carefully depicted so that we understand him as a Pakistani first and as a professional gamer second. In one of his first great victories at the tournament broadcast on Twitch, his story was very explicitly scripted and delivered to advance a particular set of interests.

In a staged video profile live streamed to hundreds of thousands of Twitch viewers, Sumail explains to his fans the lengths to which he had to travel simply to gain access to video games in his native Pakistan, as well as the trials he would later endure in his new life as an immigrant gamer in America (Figure 2.2):

> I play about nine hours a day ... Growing up I wanted to play so bad that I sold my bicycle just to play for more hours. Later, we had no

FIGURE 2.2   Sumail is depicted in this still image with the caption, "I play about nine hours a day". His singular commitment and focus on professional gaming are visible in his very concentrated gaze.

50 Encountering Gamer Citizens

car, so [my cousin] bought a small pit bike. It was only meant for one person but we got four people on it. We rode all the way to the gaming zone. Pakistan doesn't have much resources to fulfil the needs of gaming. My dad worked really hard to get me and my family to the United States. [Now] I live with eight family members in a small apartment. I share my room with three family members. *The International Championships* is everything. You win this, you win everything.

The presentation of this testimony, a combination of images from his hometown and new school life, culminates in a rather obvious attempt to both normalize and make personable the professional gamer. Sumail is portrayed as akin to any other young person struggling to find agency and purpose in the pursuit of his dream. Though perhaps playing his video game for several more hours than most (if we are to believe that he practices for nine hours per day), he is represented as having a healthy family life, parents, and siblings that work hard and wish to be supportive of his ambitions to play more and to be the best.

One of the long-lasting assertions that serves to bolster the dominant discourse of disaffection against gamers is that video games are violent.[7] Another element hidden deeper inside of that discourse is that video games are somehow an impediment to a young person's development and certainly not a productive use of one's time. Of course, there is a significant time element to playing video games, which cannot go unnoticed and should not be overlooked. Nevertheless, it is the goal of video game studios, game developers, and tournament organizers to distract from this state of affairs while simultaneously continuing to promote and distribute content that is intended to be never-ending. Thus, a complex interplay between video game development, actual video game play, and mainstream narrative scripts surrounding gaming culture sustains a fundamental (mis)understanding of gamers as wayward individuals. Corporate interests seek to establish and maintain control through the notion of a heroic, hard-working professional gamer; hence, Sumail's statement that he spends nine hours per day practicing is not only intended to valorize Esports for the Valve Corporation but also functions to elevate the live-streaming platform of Twitch, its gamer population, and streaming culture all together to a new level of respectability. Esports on Twitch is to be lauded, in this case, primarily because it makes a lot of money, and Sumail, now portrayed as a success story, confirms that through hard work, any gamer can "win big." Importantly, as an immigrant from the Third World (sic), Sumail's story confirms that you can make it in the United States if you work hard enough. In this way, Sumail serves as a poster child for the "free world" and for free enterprise through excelling at video game play.[8]

Within a circuit of culture, the video testimony of Sumail appears as a conventional media transmission, which is to say that it manifests inside a consumption chain that depends upon ongoing audience intake and corporate media output. The nodes in this segment of the circuit yield highly manufactured discursive practices, figures that are only made comprehensible as far as familiar encoding and decoding permits. For example, we can straightforwardly recognize in Sumail "the disaffected gamer," "the imperiled migrant," and similar marginalized or disadvantaged figures. These representations function on a surface level as a linear exchange from which the groundwork is established for our common understanding. However, it is possible that some consumers of Sumail's video have learned to read these preferred codes in ways that are contrary to the producers' intentions. As we shall see, viewers live streaming Sumail's mediated story may reject it as being stereotypical and even racist. The circuit of culture is therefore not an assured closed cycle of reproduction. What is in fact occurring, as in the case of Sumail, is a systemic distortion in which both the producers and consumers feedback upon each other in a non-linear exchange and a struggle over the dominant discourse. To be clear, although the video producers might wish the audience to take a certain meaning from Sumail's story, this exchange is always caught in the politics of the image. The end result of the circuit of culture is never assured, and agents on all sides of the circuit will push back, adding their own meanings and readings. Conceptually, this leaves the nodes "consumption" and "production" open to flow in unforeseen directions (Figure 2.3). Sumail helps us to witness how media consumption is never a simple passive chain of one-way communication. The circuit might be called upon to sustain dominant discourses just as easily as it may be used to reject, reverse, or overturn any predictable messaging.

ACTIVITY 1

Pause here and consider your own media consumption. This can be any form of media on any of your commonly used platforms. Do you feel in control? How does it shape you, your relationships with others, and your formulation of ideas about the world? How empowered do you feel to push back on the highly produced media that you consume each day?

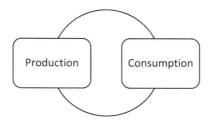

FIGURE 2.3 This diagram shows how meaning flows in both directions, from production to consumption and vice versa. These, in turn, push back against other nodes in the circuit of culture.

Civil Contracts

I have thus far raised Sumail's story without much direct reference to the audience's reaction towards him on the live stream or any further mention of the emojis that I observed in the simultaneous live chat. This is because it is important first and foremost to acknowledge how these images come to be highly reproduced as a cultural strategy in the wider context of gaming and streaming.

Ariella Azoulay offers several persuasive arguments on the visual potential and political power of images. Drawn intensely to photographs of Palestinians and to images associated with the Israeli conflict in Palestine, Azoulay proposes that these images attest to the fact of occupation, but they also demonstrate how viewers engage in a social contract based upon discourses of citizenship through images. Arriving ultimately at her landmark text, *The Civil Contract of Photography,* Azoulay warns that we easily miss this political engagement when we focus solely on an image as representation.[9] Exploring how "artistic discourse turned out to be an obstacle to seeing", Azouley suggests that this critical impasse is not a result of a failure in theoretical or scholarly rigor. Instead, it is a consequence of "image fatigue", falling prey to one's own social theorizing as acclimatization to merely spectate leads one ultimately to stop looking at media critically. More precisely, it is not necessarily that the proliferation of images now readily accessible across a myriad of media outlets is themselves impeding perception, but rather that the photograph as a prime and centuries-old example readily illustrates a slide for most of us—even for critical media theorists—into yet another "apparatus of rule". In the face of formidable "regimes of representation", as Stuart Hall phrased it, there is a mass surrender to a relentless flow of media circulation. We have turned our attention away from imagery's power to awaken our political senses; in response, Azoulay calls us back to a more fundamental civic responsibility not only of the photograph but of all images and representations.

Sumail's life story as a gamer and migrant to the U.S. is intended to shape the audience's perception of him and our "civic gaze" on him. Viewers learn something about their own citizenship and positionality as a biproduct of this media encounter. Sumail's profile video may serve for some as a slide into another apparatus of rule, i.e. some viewers may be entranced by the propagandistic messaging. Alternatively, Sumail's story might compel viewers to take these images as an invitation to formulate alternative notions and practices of citizenship. To paraphrase Azoulay, we need to look again if we are to truly see the signs of civic engagement and the outlines of citizenship in the image. The notion of the Gamer Citizen is revealed amidst this backdrop of mainstream disaffection.

Indeed, disaffection resonates consistently across media landscapes for gamers (see Chapter One). There remains, for some, a perceived decline in civic engagement and a mass resignation from formal politics altogether, yet I argue that what we are seeing in Sumail and more broadly on Twitch is a contemporary failure on the part of Twitch and the Valve Corporation to witness a new generation's performance as fundamentally political. Many individuals of all ages do feel overwhelmed by a constant stream of communication and the accelerating pace of a "High-Speed Society."[10] Rather than call this image-fatigue or a resignation of civic engagement, young people—especially gamers—are simply tired of consuming stereotypical images of their culture and are annoyed with the proliferation of such thinly veiled migration myths of the kind presented in Sumail's profile video. This is not necessarily a problem inherent to the information technologies that enable broadband communication, nor is it a democratic deficit in today's youth; rather, it is the result of misplaced and nefarious attempts by old media interests to control the dominant discourse. Sumail's video is intended to circulate unchallenged. Thus, it is time for gamers to recognize it as a corporate attempt to manipulate their media consumption, perhaps even to diminish any radical possibility for the Gamer Citizen.[11]

Mentors, Role-models, and Imperial Tracks

It is important to unpack Sumail's profile video as a case example not only because of his youth, the time he spends playing video games, or the size of his extraordinary wealth as a professional gamer (though these do figure prominently into the corporate message), but also to highlight how these aspects collectively offer the Esports industry, in this case the Valve

54 Encountering Gamer Citizens

Corporation, a conduit to maintain control over the civic potential of their images. The media producers attempt to define what it means to be a professional and upstanding gamer; they use the story of Sumail's journey to success and stardom as their focal point.

Focusing more closely upon the images of Sumail, we witness how his public persona is very carefully scripted and filled with signifiers that are deployed in a clear attempt to render gamers as revered rather than scorned in the public eye. Notably, this is an attempt to encourage gamers, many of whom are ardent fans of Sumail, to not only follow in the footsteps of their professional idols but, more importantly, to invest their own gameplay labour into this burgeoning industry, to spend more of their time and money on competitive video games, and to invest monetarily into gaming and streaming.

There are multiple references to Sumail's racial background in his profile video. We witness him proclaiming that "Pakistan doesn't have much resources to fulfil the needs of gaming" and "I live with eight family members". While they may evoke a certain embodied empathy for a professional gamer, Sumail's testimony conspicuously helps communicate a story that is articulated in terms of race, class, and migration. Such a "rags to riches" story cannot be separated from its imperial implications. Indeed, the profile is indicative of a more widespread phenomenon, a venture to define a gamer nation as one that operates like a colonial power to bring together gamers from around the world—not simply to "be together from wherever they play" as is the official Twitch marketing tagline, but also to now leave behind a gamer life of relative isolation and squalor, to find a rich new cyberspace, a whole new land of opportunity, and, vitally, a space that can only be granted as charity from a more advanced culture.[12] It is significant that, as scripted, Sumail could not rise to become a champion all on his own. Instead, his profile video stresses his need to be saved in order to be welcomed into his new home and respected within his gaming community.

Later in the live stream, we learn of Sumail's older and more experienced teammate, Clinton Loomis. Loomis, notably an older white American man, is cast as the veteran player who helps to coach Sumail in his new country and to stay motivated as a member of his top-division Esports team (Figure 2.4).

There were several responses to this story that reveal not only a racial and colonial faultline but also how corporate messages can be contested in nuanced ways. Conceivably, Sumail should be celebrated as an example of a young person who has excelled in his field, winning large sums of prize money on his journey towards achieving a gaming version of the "American Dream." It might be that we should commend his outstanding efforts

Encountering Gamer Citizens 55

FIGURE 2.4 Sumail is pictured here walking and talking with his team captain, Clinton. He expresses how much he has learned from his team and how he could not have come this far without help.

in the face of adversity and in a profession that is currently even shorter-lived than he is. Alternatively, his story might simply deserve attention as a positive role model representing a young digital generation. What gets lost in each of these framings is a consideration of what the carefully constructed narrative accomplishes when circulated on the Twitch platform. Sumail's story is one that depends upon messages and images that inform and shape the public's imagination of him. These, in turn, mostly find their meaning and expression through intertextual relationships exchanged and mediated on the stream. "The Young Sumail," as Valve would have us come to know him, may represent a great many things to a great number of people, but his public persona as it continues to be encoded and decoded by audiences remains unfixed and a point of contestation. On the day we watched his profile video and subsequent victory match, there was no readily observable consensus on who Sumail was or what he should stand for in a figurative gamer nation. In fact, as we shall see, much of the vast Twitch population viewed his profile as idealistically contrived and met it with significant resistance.

Before proceeding with our analysis of Sumail, it is important to reflect on his place in the cultural circuit. The Valve Corporation seeks to redefine the boundaries of acceptability for gamers and to broadcast Sumail as an Esports success story. We witness this as a form of imperialist control, since the images of Sumail and his teammate Loomis impose a regulated gamer body that is understood to be professional and championed only if it assumes the characteristics and responsibilities of model citizenry. A gamer like Sumail, who notably follows in Loomis' footsteps, must be charitable, must live fruitfully in his community, and must always act in

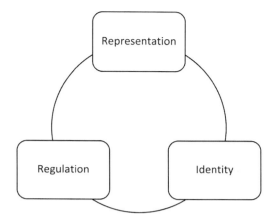

FIGURE 2.5 The three nodes of the circuit of culture, "regulation," "representation", and "identity" contribute to a space of flows, supporting and sometimes competing for cultural understanding.

support of his fellow gamers. Within the circuit, the node we called "regulation" comes up against friction from its neighbouring nodes, "representation" and "identity" (Figure 2.5). Each node in the circuit contributes as well as competes for our common cultural understanding. Recall that "regulation" in a circuit of culture implies all the powers that enable communication, and in the case of Sumail, this includes but is not limited to regulations of corporate origin. There exists, in addition, a whole network of codes that historically shapes our understanding from the outside, and this feeds back in and between the nodes "representation" and "identity".

Opening the Circuit

Complicating this process, enter emojis as new "floating signifiers", opening up the circuit of culture in nuanced ways. Sumail's video was revealed to be enmeshed in a complex exchange and flurry of messages from viewers responding in the live chat (Figure 2.6).

We can come to a deeper understanding of the critique contained in these messages through an analysis of how communicative tones are commonly conveyed over Twitch. Despite their commenting in apparent jest, viewers in the live chat were clearly agitated. This was made visible through an intricate system of emojis that convey highly localized meaning. Chief among these is the "BibleThump"—an emoji originating from the video game *The Binding of Isaac* (not at all associated with Sumail's tournament) and widely used to express strong emotions with regards to content on livestreams. Emojis represent an evolving language for gamers

Encountering Gamer Citizens 57

FIGURE 2.6 Gamers respond in a flurry of messages containing complex and coded language, including a number of popular emojis.

on Twitch, where millions of emojis are circulated daily.[13] They exhibit a living history of gaming, often drawing from original references to previously popular streamed video games, with the BibleThump standing out as a crowd favourite; in fact, it has become so widely used on Twitch, and for so long, that few gamers would question its intended meaning, or even remember where it came from. There are hundreds, if not thousands, of similar emojis in circulation, but only a small handful are free to use by anyone on the platform, and fewer still have grown to be so completely emblematic of the community "writ large" that they have been elevated into a category of common daily usage.

During my time in the field, I found that the high usage of BibleThump occurs within the gamer community as a form of self-reference to a hyper-awareness of emotional frustration. On the other hand, gamers are also cognizant of mainstream challenges to the authenticity of such public declarations. "Video games aren't real", "watching people play video games sounds ridiculous", or "how could anyone enjoy spending their time doing anything like that!?" are just a few responses in a chorus from the dominant discourse that builds upon an increasingly common sentiment. This routine dismissal of gamers and gaming (now also streaming) has inspired a form of self-reflexivity within the wider Twitch community. Gamers manifest a critique in their chat interaction and their use of the BibleThump to react to what is occurring, as well as to make a meta-statement about what is happening in the evolution and mainstream receptions of gaming culture more generally.

The use of BibleThump shows that gamers do in fact have feelings and, in the case of Sumail, that they refuse to have those feelings manipulated. In the following instance, the criticism is directly named with reference to yet another trope from Sumail's migration testimony (Figure 2.7).

Not to be interpreted as a form of sympathy or empathy for Sumail (who reportedly had to sell his bicycle to afford his computer in Pakistan), this user in chat does not support the claim; rather, in this case, emojis serve as a calling out of video producers for what appeared to be a contrived and shameless attempt to win the hearts and minds of gamers. Together with the apparent corporate insincerity, BibleThump testifies to Sumail's background story as an insult to those in the actual gaming communities who might be struggling to afford the rising costs of new equipment. Circumstances seemed so contrived in the profile that Sumail's story simply could not possibly be believed, thus BibleThump is intended as a reclamation of Twitch. It is a statement affirming that the streaming website ought to reflect the sincere interests and realities of real gamers, not corporate interests.

FIGURE 2.7   This is one reaction among many responding to the incredible story of Sumail having to sell his bicycle to afford a new gaming computer in Pakistan.

The skeptical position in chat was made even clearer as more clues streamed in, and a complex intertextual story was gradually revealed both in text form and through the use of emojis. "NOT AGAIN!", the gamers in attendance proclaimed loudly. In a hidden message of disgust from gamers, still other Twitch emojis were deployed, for example, Dansgame, the face of a popular streamer and the principal emote to communicate anger or antipathy. Viewers also remarked on using the less enthusiastic ResidentSleeper, another extremely common emoji used to express disinterest, boredom, or exhaustion.[14] These emojis formulate a nascent critique; that is to say, they constitute an informal charge against the Valve Corporation and Twitch. Both are found guilty of manipulation towards their core gamer audience and responsible for the betrayal of their once loyal consumer base. The corporate motivation behind Sumail's story was indeed not very well disguised. Gamers understood this to be a disingenuous attempt to render Esports as venerable in the eyes of a wider public. What is more, for those in attendance on the live stream, this was not only a distasteful display but an altogether unacceptable framing of Sumail, whose images were clearly being leveraged to capture more market share.

Such a pattern of resistance in and through emojis on the live chat is the start of emojis being utilized as a form of civic duty. It demonstrates the rise of a Gamer Citizen who is fundamentally anti-corporate as well as anti-imperialist, all while remaining intensely committed to protecting the interests and wellbeing of fellow gamer compatriots. Not all responses, however, proved quite so progressive, and they were certainly not entirely innocuous. Sumail and his manufactured profile exposed longstanding and apparently racial divides in the gaming community. As I suggested, Sumail's depiction as a gamer of color needing assistance from his elder white teammate, Clinton, was taken by several streamers as an opportunity to amplify the racialized corporate script, typifying Sumail together with other gamers of color to dehumanize and shame rather than elevate them.

The "Anele" emoji is the face of Twitch Partnerships Lead Anele Andeshmand. He is a permanent Twitch staff person working for the website, and, as with others discussed above, his likeness is used very widely on the platform as a symbol and shorthand for lively communication. The difference from the other emojis discussed above, however, is how the Anele emoji—notably a depiction of him wearing a turban—is primarily deployed across the wider Twitch as an attempt to maintain a racial hierarchy. Despite the emoji originally being used within Anele's home community as a supportive characterization of his unique gamer persona, the Anele emoji in the context of Sumail's story

FIGURE 2.8   The Anele emoji is seen being used in conjunction with symbols that depict the terrorist attacks on the United States on September 11th, 2001.

cannot easily be defended as an affirmation of a diverse gamer identity. Far from being an invitation to bring more gamers of color into a robust community online, Anele serves, as we see in the profile video of Sumail, largely to subordinate, to reduce, and to divide. Through Anele, Sumail becomes a social signifier that represents threatening racial difference; at its most extreme, his likeness is read as a terrorist and an outsider (Figure 2.8).

The symbolism, if not immediately clear, suggests that Sumail and Anele, or any brown gamer for that matter, are to be understood as a threat akin to those who flew planes into the World Trade Centre on September 11th, 2001. Although this example is not intended as a literal juxtaposition, the subtext of subordination and vilification nevertheless serves to keep Sumail and other gamers like him at a distance, a reminder not to forget where they come from and how they will never fully belong.

Conclusion: "Emojis as Civic Duty"

In closing, I remark on the emergence of "emojis as civic duty", which is to conceptualize gamer's use of emoji on streams as a political responsibility and central agency for the figure of the Gamer Citizen. Firstly, even to suggest such a thing is to invite longstanding debates and fervently defended ideals of what constitutes a political subject or, for that matter, what qualifies as citizenship. Politics immediately implies certain openings in the context of Sumail, not least those aspects of his migration story that directly reference his movements from one nation, Pakistan, to another, the United States. Yet my purpose in raising this case study and the subsequent analysis has more to do with an inquiry into something alternatively positioned. The response to Sumail's profile brings with it ramifications beyond strict geopolitics. While there is a plethora of scholars who would argue that affairs involving race and migration such as these are inexorably linked, my purpose in this chapter is to focus on emojis themselves with regards to the question of how gamers engage politically within a circuit of culture. Emojis on live streams testify to the fact of socio-political and geographical occupations of a familiar colonial

Encountering Gamer Citizens **61**

and corporate kind, but for a gaming community, they also render an entirely different perspective with new potentialities for cultural representation.

Emojis, upon closer reading in this case, lead one to consider an evolution of gaming culture but more forcefully a revolution of media and communication that is informed by a particular gamer's history in parallel with an extended political and contemporary world. We are witnessing in Emojis the trappings of the figure of Gamer Citizen, and this is accomplished through disruptions and even occasional confirmations that actual gamers leverage towards the dominant discourse. As already suggested, the circuit of culture is a space of non-linear flows where meaning is given and meaning is taken across distinct nodes, but the circuit is only ever completed and effective when it is understood within a historical context of dominance. The circuit is always historically determined; thus, we see race-based discrimination against Sumail. Each instance of this condemnable activity is a reminder that there are durable and insidious "floating signifiers" of the dominant racial and imperial hierarchies from history long past yet ever present.

Nevertheless, such signifiers on the live stream are only relatively fixed moments. Emojis like the BibleThump, Dansgame, and ResidentSleeper are powerful representations that evoke some measure of resistance to dominance, each constituting its own break or interruption in the passage of communication forms.[15] These emojis constitute "emojis as civic duty" in a circuit of culture, which is to argue that they operate relatively detached from the established circuit while nevertheless holding the radical possibility of shaping each node. Emojis are massively popular, and their increasing usage amongst gamers on Twitch gives hope for an evolving Gamer Citizen.

ACTIVITY 2

Consider your own "circuit of culture." On a sheet of paper, fill in what is involved at each of the nodes in your circuit. Who are the agents of power at each node? What are the important factors to consider?

Although I focus on the case study of Sumail in this chapter, there are many other recent examples that one could highlight in order to draw out a richer discussion of civic responsibility among gamers. Through Sumail, we witness how gamers of color may find success in a corporate world by striking what is sometimes called a "hegemonic bargain".[16] Sumail

62 Encountering Gamer Citizens

has joined the live-streaming scene and has struck a deal with Valve and Twitch, working with his teammates to become more identifiable as a professional Esports champion and more accepted by his peers. Yet gamers like Sumail still have further challenges to face. His racial differences are coded through his migration video and the emojis that circulate through the live chat. Only when he is supposedly helped by his gamer teammate, Clinton Loomis, does he learn the values and virtues of citizenship and take on new responsibilities in his new home. This narrative, in the circuit of culture, renders an interplay between the nodes of "production" and "consumption" that is non-linear and contributes to an opportunity for critical growth amongst gamers on Twitch. And yet, gamers are notoriously difficult to control. They push back on "regulation," "representation," and "identity" through their lively chat interactions and their rich use of emojis on stream.

As the continued derogatory use of "Anele" [🐵] suggests, Sumail is never fully admitted into the gaming community, yet there is evidence that some gamers are tired of migration myths and corporate stereotypical messaging and are at least partly ready to step outside of their habituated character. It remains to be seen if gamers are fully able to reorganize these streaming domains, which both enable and constrain citizenship. Citizenship in the 21st century is a question of how people enact themselves and how they negotiate rights, duties, and daily responsibilities as they now extend online as well as offline. This has traditionally been facilitated under the scope and purview of nation-states, but now it must be understood as extending into virtual worlds. Emojis now help to establish that virtual social and symbolic order. They enable some gamers to stake "break out" claims, holding out hope for a more progressive and inclusive future, while they also sustain established racist and imperialist scripts deeply embedded within the nodes of the historic circuit.

QUESTIONS

1. Why is it important that we learn to witness rather than merely play the role of spectator in our media consumption?
2. What might be the significance of an "emoji code"?
3. Are gamers free to push back on dominant discourses? Do we see the rise of a more inclusive and responsible Gamer Citizen emerging online using emojis?

Notes

1 Stuart Hall, "The Work of Representation," in *Representation: Cultural Representations and Signifying Practices*. London: Sage 1997, 15–30. 'Floating signifiers' reference in Nathan Grayson, "Twitch Chat Racism Changed Hearthstone Pro Terrence Miller's Career." *Kotaku.com*, 10 July 2016, https://kotaku.com/hearthstone-pro-terrence-miller-hopes-to-clean-up-twitc-1787551043 (accessed 06 February 2022)

2 Marcel Danesi, The Semiotics of Emoji: The rise of visual language in the age of the internet. Bloomsbury 2019, 45.

3 Marengo, D., Fabrizia Giannotta, Michele Settanni, "Assessing personality using emoji: An exploratory study" in *Personality an Individual Differences* 2017, 112: 74–78.

4 Miller, H., Daniel Kluver, Jacob Thebault-Spieker, Loren Terveen, Brent Hecht, "Understanding Emoji Ambiguity in Context: The Role of Text in Emoji-Related Miscommunication" in *Association for the Advancement of Artificial Intelligence*, 2017.

5 The traditional effects of emojis are best explored in: Miller et al, "Understanding Emoji Ambiguity in Context: The Role of Text in Emoji-Related Miscommunication"; Ljubesic, N. and Darja Fiser, "A Global Analysis of Emoji Usage" in *Proceedings of the 10th Web as Corpus Workshop (WAC-X) and the EmpiriST Shared Task* 2016, pages 82–89; Stark, L. and Kate Crawford, "The Conservatism of Emoji: Work, Affect, and Communication" in *Social Media + Society* July–December 2015: 1–11.

6 Hall, *Cultural Representations and Signifying Practices*; Stuart Hall, "Encoding, decoding." In: During, S (ed.) *The Cultural Studies Reader*. London: Routledge 1991, 90–103.

7 Joseph R. Dominick, "Videogames, Television Violence, and Aggression in Teenagers" in *Journal of Communication* Vol 34, Issue 2, 1984, 136–147.

8 I use the term "Third World" intentionally as the phrase captures what I believe the producers of this profile intended.

9 Ariella Azoulay, The Civil Contract of Photography, Zone Books New York 2008, 11. All Azoulay quotes from this source unless noted.

10 Judy Wajcman, "Pressed for Time: The Acceleration of Life" in Digital Capitalism 2016.

11 Megan Boler warns in her text how spectating signifies learned and chosen modes of visual omission and erasure. This dangerous as it completely prevents important forms of critical thinking in education. See: Feeling Power: Emotions and Education. Routledge 1999, 184.

12 Cruickshand, J. & Patricia Grimshaw, "Indigenous Land Loss, Justice and Race: Ann Bon and the Contradictions of Settler Humanitarianism." Eds. Z Laidlaw, Alan Lester in *Indigenous Communities and Settler Colonialism*: MPS Limited 2015.

13 Twitch Stats, https://twitchtracker.com/statistics (accessed 10 August, 2021)

14 "ResidentSleeper"; This is the face of Oddler. Oddler is a streamer on Twitch and was doing a 72-hour Resident Evil marathon stream when he fell asleep about 66 hours into his broadcast. His sleeping stream became massively popular and at one point the viewer count even reached 13,000 users in chat (twitch.tv/oddler).

15 Hall, "Encoding, decoding," 118.

16 Anthony Chen, "Lives at the Center of the Periphery, Lives at the Periphery of the Center: Chinese American Masculinities and Bargaining with Hegemony." in *Gender and Society*, 13–5, 1999, 584–607.

3
NOT A GAME

Introduction

Video games can be deeply nostalgic for many. They often evoke a wide range of emotions, sometimes pleasant and other times unpleasant. Gamers are frequently joyful but also, on occasion, anxious, even mournful, for their worlds, avatars, and friends of a bygone time. Nostalgia, or in this case, yearning for a lost happiness in games, is perhaps one of the most commonly expressed emotions. Even those who no longer play video games often recall with fondness their early years playing a favourite title. In Chapter 1, I looked critically at the "magic circle", understanding it as a video game theory that narrowly emphasizes how gamers relate to others and to video games because it primarily emphasizes relationships that are determined by the confines of virtual worlds. Gamers, in this view, are not understood as having intense relationships, relevant knowledge, or even political expertise in a world outside of video games, a lack of sophistication attributed to their being undeveloped learners. In this chapter, I acknowledge that virtual spaces, characteristics, and relationships of video games remain of deep consequence for gamers, but I also argue that live-video streams on Twitch show us how gaming and streaming are not a mere retreat into virtual worlds; rather, they are an affective encounter between gamers that is rarely seen from other prevailing perspectives. I establish an important premise in this chapter, namely that gamers do in fact form relationships with each other and that their responsibility towards each other, even in conflict, extends beyond the virtual confines of video games.

DOI: 10.4324/9781003341079-4

The following brief exchange between gamers represents a moment of nostalgia exchanged on Twitch:

Viewer298: Where did you get your icon for Twitch?
Broadcaster: My icon is something a friend drew for me. It's my character in a game I used to play.

The viewer is inquiring about the broadcaster's profile icon image, which out of context seems like an innocuous enough query, but more specifically, the viewer is curious about how such an enigmatic as well as stylized avatar was chosen. The channel hosting this interaction was a stream dedicated exclusively to the gameplay and commentary of the video game *Super Mario 64*. It had grown into a community where gamers could gather mostly for the express purpose of discussions, reminiscences, and, in general, celebration of the video game character Mario. Often, the most successful streams (and certainly some of the most populated) are those that feature retro and highly recognizable video games. Gamers report on how they gather on Twitch not just because they do not have the time or money to play the latest titles but because they miss playing those beloved older video games—games that they perhaps lost the opportunity to play when they were newly available on the market or games that had been lost over the years. Gamers sometimes long for the feeling of playing in abandoned virtual worlds, and this is reflected in the high traffic one often witnesses gathering on any given retro-based Twitch stream. What stands out most in the brief exchange, however, is how this streamer of a channel dedicated to the much beloved character of Mario could simultaneously show so much pride in a completely different character from a long-forgotten and obscure alternative title. Many of us on the stream at the time were tuning in to witness the amazing feats of Mario gameplay. We were not expecting this other character. We did not recognize who this profile picture was meant to depict, yet we would soon discover that this was a work of art that had been drawn by a friend to resemble an avatar from a very niche Japanese series called *Gakuen Hetalia*. Perplexed, I wondered what made this character so valuable? More significantly, who was this friend who drew the image? Suffice it to say that on Twitch, gamers often want to learn the details of such minutia that extend beyond the immediately apparent boundaries of any given game at play.

This chapter reports on the early days of my fieldwork on Twitch, the purpose of which was not simply to document recent trends in gaming but also to challenge my own assumptions and expectations about what gamer communities more precisely stood for. Gamers, I believed, were not the disaffected people described elsewhere; their social activities online could

66 Not a Game

prove instead their rather devoted and supportive nature. I wanted, therefore, to test my hypothesis that there could be more to gaming than that which is established within the confines of video game play. It is important to emphasize from the very start that live streaming on Twitch is *not a game*, hence the title of this chapter, and that the several streams on which I met with participants to observe and discuss their use of the website both for broadcasting and for viewing video games involved multiple and varied relationships.

The chapter takes on the following trajectory. First, I describe my very first days entering the field, which I began by viewing and participating in a live stream by a gamer called Yinfay. I frame this early encounter as a process of finding home for its significance as a multilayered metaphor that was directly embedded into how Yinfay perceived her own community activity—she routinely described her stream as both a community and a home—but also to describe this vital stage of my entering into participant observation. I was quite literally trying to find my own way into a new home on Twitch, both as a researcher and as a gamer. Second, I describe how Yinfay would also be broadcasting her final stream before taking a lengthy break. Yinfay was preparing to go on vacation, yet this moment of farewell proved to be a unique opportunity to further explore a gamer's responsibility to themselves and, more importantly, to uncover a gamers' responsibility towards others. Yinfay was deeply distressed. As perhaps anyone might feel before departing on a long trip away from their normal work routine, she struggled with a degree of apprehension; in her particular case, this was compounded by the thought of abandoning the people she cared for most in her daily life—her followers and viewers on Twitch. In the final section of the chapter, I share how feelings of establishing a warm and welcoming home on Twitch are not necessarily sentiments shared by all in the community. I explore a moment upon Yinfay's return where distinct agitators inundated the stream, demonstrating how communities are also sometimes struggled over as well as defended.

Collectively, the ethnographic accounts of this chapter show a form of gamer agency and activity going beyond the coded parameters of the video game. These moments are emblematic of the kind of responsibilities and interpersonal strife one might expect to find in any home and amidst any social collective in a digital age.

Finding Home

Yinfay was the first of my participants to enthusiastically join on the project for this book, working in collaboration with me prior to the start of my initial participant observation and even before I had the chance to enter her channel for the first time. She volunteered several of her preliminary insights via personal messages and emails after I initially reached out. In that first correspondence, she was so keen to share information about her knowledge of streaming activity that she proactively offered to put me in touch with other streamers with whom she was in contact and who were working on a separate network project. From the start, Yinfay exhibited a keen intellectual drive that was equaled by her personal and professional commitment to her community channel—her "home" as she called it. To her, Twitch was a place where anyone could find a refuge from the more chaotic and stressful aspects of daily life. I would discover that being at home for Yinfay would mean partly inhabiting the video game *Guild Wars 2* and playing on a game mode that was commonly called "sPvP" (structured Player versus Player), which is a type of game play involving two groups engaged in combat in a multiplayer online battle arena style setting.

To end my introduction of Yinfay at the mere mention of *Guild Wars 2* and at such a meagre description of sPvP, however, would not only do a disservice to her earnest efforts to contribute to the research for this book, but it would also be a waste of her gift of such an open invitation to learn more about the everyday life of gamers. On the second day of my observation, I found Yinfay's stream title concisely phrased. "Spvp Guardian burst" was to indicate to her viewers that her intended focus for the day was to share a form of sPvP and teach others about her individual style of gameplay utilizing the guardian character class.

Guild Wars 2 has several different subcategories of character classes and professions, with the guardian being marketed as a paragon of virtue capable of both dispatching enemy threats quickly by dealing significantly high "burst damage" while concurrently providing support to allies and friends. Deploying hallmark skills in the game such as "Shelter", which is to block attacks while healing, and "Sanctuary", which is a protective healing barrier for allies preventing foes and projectiles from entering, Yinfay's metaphor of building a home on Twitch quite literally extended to her choice of characters for the virtual battlefield. Players tended to struggle in a way to find stable ground within an otherwise chaotic and dangerous game mode, and Yinfay was equipped to help them.

Guild Wars 2, in fact, has many different internal game types, but the sPvP variant tends to be among the most competitive as well as the most populated. Players in this mode enjoy significantly higher priority status allocated by the game developers to receive balance updates and bug fixes. The objective on the surface of this mode seems deceptively clear: two teams of five players are meant to vie for the highest score or to be the first to obtain 500 points in a 15-minute game of conquest. As I observed

68 Not a Game

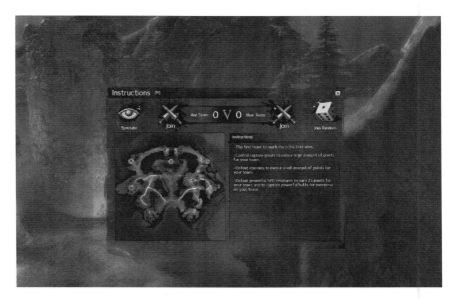

FIGURE 3.1 sPvP world map.

Yinfay's stream with only a passing knowledge of these details, I soon discovered that this game was far more complex. Split across three battle zones, Yinfay and her teammates proceeded to capture these zones and defend against the opposing team. The game awards points according to how long a player or group of players hold the zones on the map. In addition, players gain extra credit for any successful accomplishment of secondary objectives, such as killing an enemy opponent or apprehending another of the arena's special mechanical objectives (Figure 3.1).

Like an evolution or hybrid somewhere between competitive high-speed chess and championship boxing, Yinfay and her teammates each kept an eye on their respective mini maps, determining which zones were being held and which might be more open to capture next. At times, there was a direct route to victory by challenging an opponent with superior fighting skills in the form of crosses and jabs. At other times, they moved as a unit to complete auxiliary targets, mirroring the opposing team's movements and applying strategic pressure, almost resembling a "Petrov's Defense" in chess.[1]

On top of the technical aspects, there is a distinct beauty to the world of sPvP, a graphical fidelity extending across each of the realms in *Guild wars 2*, including displays of familiar yet uniquely stylized medieval art themes. Glamour in the form of thousands of armour and weapon skins, including fantasy outfits and celebration tonics, lends a visual appeal that

FIGURE 3.2 Beautifully rendered world with fighting avatars.

is embraced by players of all sorts, including the many who never step foot into a competitive match.[2] From the screen capture of a skirmish occurring on a capture zone (Figure 3.2), one can get a sense of the importance of artwork and graphics design to the game. Coniferous trees with mountain ranges are visible in the distant background; flowers and weeds—even blades of grass—gather just outside the zone; there are clouds in the sky with blooms of light reflecting off the metallic surfaces of the armour and weaponry. Finally, there are the player characters themselves, depicted with such nuance of expression as to suggest the complexity of animation and the broad range of movement available in each confrontation.

As her match continued, Yinfay cut herself off from her own Twitch commentary. We, the viewers in the live chat, now watched as Yinfay focused more intensely on winning her battle at one of three capture zones in the *Forest of Niflhel*, as the arena was called. "Oh my God this is …" She remarked suddenly. Her guardian player character was locked in single combat against an opponent warrior character, and the battle was turning against her. "No no no! No no no! The sphere! The sphere! Oh my God no …" Yinfay called out with urgency, directing her teammates with instructions and hoping to warn them of an enemy that was approaching on one of the unique objectives called simply "the sphere". Voice communication between teammates is normally not a primary feature available to players in *Guild Wars 2*. Such third-party voice capability is instead left up to the players themselves to make use of voice-over-the-internet protocol (VOIP) software. Yinfay and some of her allies used an application called *TeamSpeak*, which formed yet another floor in Yinfay's metaphorical home.

70 Not a Game

Yinfay's desperate cries for help were directed towards her team. "No one is coming?" Yinfay asked as she was about to suffer imminent defeat at the hands of an enemy warrior character. Yinfay's teammate is heard apologizing for not responding in time: "Sorry I was fighting at middle and then I got outnumbered so I had to disengage", he explains to Yinfay, adding that he was also caught on another point where several enemy players were heavily engaged. There is frustration and resignation in Yinfays voice as she responds "It's okay … I don't know where our teammates are, and I feel constantly outnumbered …" Yinfay and her teammates ultimately lost their match, but even in defeat, they would have each other as solace. We, the teams on voice communications as well as several hundred more holding fast in the live chat on Twitch, were each dwelling together with Yinfay at "home". This was a collective that one can rightly call a community, with agency and responsibility towards each other now spanning well beyond the original confines of the originally coded virtual world.

ACTIVITY 1

1. Take a moment to reflect on a multiplayer game that you are familiar with. What are the rules of this game? How is it played? Now think about the context of play. Where is the game played? With Whom?
2. When do communities of gamers emerge in support of multiplayer games? Why do they form? Is it for competition or cooperation? Is it for learning game strategy? How might communities of multiplayer games stand for something beyond the limits of the video games they are premised upon?

More Shapes

In the early 1990s, Howard Rheingold famously identified important features of what he called "virtual community". As he described it, virtual communities are "social aggregations that emerge from the Net when enough people carry on public discussions for long enough, with sufficient human feeling, to form webs of personal relationships in cyberspace".[3] People may not meet face-to-face, but they can nevertheless share interests and intimacies through the internet. I praise Rheingold's writing on his experiences with what was commonly called computer-mediated communication (CMC). His work is an early recognition of the nature of communities that are formed when people interact socially online. What is more, his insights lead directly to an argument in support of the researcher/ethnographer who is engaged in deep contact in the field and who narrativizes based upon observations, thus sharing new experiences, communicating feelings, and building knowledge. We call this important practice "participant observation". Notably, such a method is the key to making any pronouncements about a community, be it virtual or otherwise.

During an interview in *Life on The Electronic Frontier*, Rheingold recalls how he first went online in the early 1980s because he "really wanted to connect with other people".[4] As a writer, he had grown familiar with his computer as a tool for productivity and for work. Though he found himself sceptical of using the technology as a means for social connection, he set out regardless to socialize online and to find his way into a second "home" amongst his fellow cyber-inhabitants. In his numerous celebrated publications, Rheingold describes all this in greater detail, along with other notable accounts about the early internet.[5] His enduring sentiments are captured best in the following passage:

I routinely meet people and get to know them months or years before I see them—one of the ways my world today is a different world, with different friends and different concerns, from the world I experienced in premodem days. The places I visit in my mind, and **the people I communicate** with from one moment to the next, are entirely different from the content of my thoughts or the state of my circle of friends before **I started dabbling in virtual communities**. One minute I'm involved in the minutiae of local matters such as planning next week's bridge game, and the next minute **I'm part of a debate raging in seven countries**. Not only do I inhabit my virtual communities; to the degree that I carry around their conversations in my head and begin to mix it up with them in real life, **my virtual communities also inhabit my life. I've been colonized; my sense of family at the most fundamental level has been virtualized** (my emphasis added).[6]

It is important to take Rheingold's testimony into account as we witness the building of communities online in contemporary times. The current research for this book involved significantly more than mere "dabbling in" a virtual community. It also did not quite resemble the same profound transformation or colonization of the self that Rheingold describes in what was then termed "cyberspace". I did not develop a new sense of family, and I certainly was not virtualized to any degree during my time on Twitch. Such superlative descriptions about life online seem almost quaint on today's internet. Nevertheless, it must be reported that live streaming continues to be premised on forging a deep level of human contact. Through Yinfay's

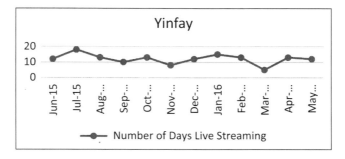

FIGURE 3.3 Yinfay's streaming activity.

open participation and her first-hand experience competing in sPvP, we come to see in increasing detail the complexity, if not the significance of this modern-day CMC. Over the roughly one year that I spent following Yinfay, I witnessed fluctuations in her streaming activity across numerous days going live on Twitch (Figure 3.3). It was during this protracted period that I came to a deeper appreciation not only of her dedicated efforts to live stream consistently but also of her long-term energies to maintain her "home". Day in and day out, hundreds of others routinely tuned in, and I would ultimately graduate into feeling some version of co-habitation with Yinfay. By the end of my observations, I considered myself to be a part of this "virtual community", even if I was only to play a minor part (Figure 3.4).

FIGURE 3.4 Be part of the community!

While I show regard for Rheingold on the power and significance of virtual community, I acknowledge the validity of arguments by some of his mounting critics who disapprove of his often exaggerated and overly positive framing. Rheingold affirms perhaps too hastily the "frontier" aspects of his relationships online (a term with problematic historical connotations), and he appears to offer even less regard for the actualities of what expenses it takes to sustain networked connections of this kind, or the privilege held by early users of the internet.[7] Briefly responding to these objections, I would simply state that most early accounts of technological progress are fuelled by considerable celebration and enthusiasm. This is a characteristic response found not only in Rheingold but also in his numerous contemporaries; Nicholas Negroponte and the early works of Sherry Turkle, for example, also mirrored the same hopefulness and similarly aligned utopianism in their acclaimed accounts of "being digital" and "life on the screen".[8] The first scholars on the scene of new technical phenomena tend to articulate a sort of dichotomous or binary model of thinking about the real and the virtual. They see great promise in the virtual world because they wish it to become a sort of successor. They imagine that cyberspace, or the internet, as we call it today, might one day bring some level of balance and stability to our everyday life where hardship and injustice outwardly persist and seem insurmountable.

Still new magic circles emerge in place of old ones wherever alternative theorizations are developed using hybrid virtual/real world logics. As it happens, the theoretical backdrop from early internet studies arrives near the founding simultaneously of online gaming studies. Gaming too was initially understood as resting upon magical properties very much resembling the notion of virtual community; the magic circle of gaming is a virtual space that ostensibly circumscribes gamers as they are radically transported as well as transformed (see Chapter 1).

Searching for an update to this theorizing, Rene Glas et al. build upon Goffman's "social frame theory", offering a study of video games to be taken up in terms of "frames" rather than a single and fragile magic circle.[9] They argue that a theory of magic circles is lacking in theoretical cohesion precisely because it imposes such sharp divisions between what is considered real and what is merely contained in the realm of play.[10] Frames enable a freer-flowing consideration of new emergent activities or frames within frames that are distinct in their particularities, showing how gamers create and maintain their social order through the support of their many layered interactions. This new theory, deploying frames to describe the distinctive modes of play, brings into focus a profoundly social environment. We are better equipped to understand contemporary online gaming through the use of frames as well as their various keys because we

74 Not a Game

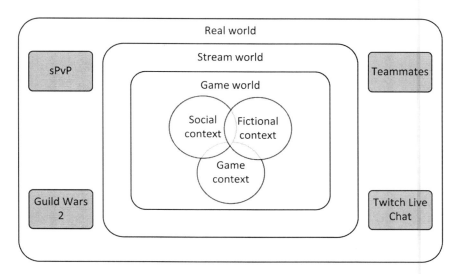

FIGURE 3.5 Frame diagram of Yinfay's stream world.

can subsequently use this framework to de-emphasize the common trope of gaming as an escape from the real world, building instead a richer form of situated knowledge about this human activity system.

On this type of view, the game world is contained within the real world, and within that container reside many related contexts of play. Adjusted to the example of Yinfay, consider the frame diagram (Figure 3.5).

Figure 3.5 is an illustration of different aspects of Yinfay's live stream and how they interact within the space of frames. Goffman describes how, in our daily life, a series of frames come together to organize our activities and thereby structure our experiences. These frames combine with various keys to provide "a crucial role in determining what we think is really going on".[11] Notice how each frame in the diagram is contained within the single larger frame called "real world". Each frame, including "stream world", "game world", and the various sub-contexts of play, exists as an integral element and not a separate part outside of this rendering of a complete reality.

Yinfay is playing as previously described within the beautifully rendered and medieval-styled video game *Guild Wars 2*. She is playing, more precisely, in the competitive game mode called sPvP, which requires our consideration of all the complexity, rules, and objectives developed therein. While these two keys might initially indicate a strong connection only to the frame "game world" and perhaps secondarily to the frame "stream world", we ought to acknowledge how these also remain elsewhere permanently affixed. Though Yinfay is engaged in gaming and streaming, she is also strongly rooted in reality through her communication with her teammates and her simultaneous engagements with those of us participating in the live chat. Put simply, streaming video games on Twitch—and this goes equally for many social interactions over the internet—is not an escape or transportation away to alternative domains. Instead, these interactive experiences are extensions of the real world—frames within frames—that sometimes come to form a vital part of peoples' everyday lives.

ACTIVITY 2

1 Use the following template to construct your own frame analysis of a video game streaming community. Fill in each of the blank keys exhibited as grey boxes for your analysis. Consider how the keys in your template come to shape the experiences of peoples' everyday lives.

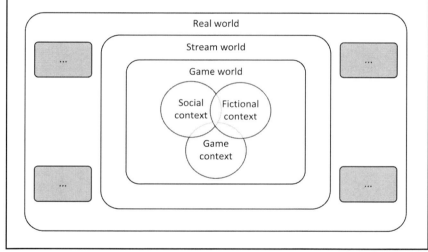

Going on Holiday

A few months into participant observation, Yinfay informed her stream that she would be going on holiday and that she would not be returning for several days. The stream had only gone live for a few minutes (just 35 viewers accumulated in chat), but several concerned viewers immediately inquired about her destination as well as the date of her return. Clearly saddened to be leaving, as was apparent by the tone of her voice, Yinfay

76 Not a Game

explained her agenda for the day, conveying at the same time her deep concern for interrupting her regular broadcasts:

May 31 14:27:54 <Formedking27>	where are you going?
May 31 14:27:56 <CoolidgetHD>	you going away Yinfay?
May 31 14:27:58 <TheKuroShin>	When you back?
May 31 14:28:20 <Yinfay *VOICE COMMENT*>	So I'm going to play Guild Wars 2. I'm going to do some dungeons. I have to do dungeons with both the EU and North America [servers] because I want to make everyone happy and because I'm going on holiday and I can't stream while I'm gone. I'm going to miss you guys so much!

In addition to sPvP, there are several other modes within the game *Guild Wars 2*. A second very popular mode, and the one that Yinfay was promising to play, did not involve competitive combat against other players. Instead, a single group of five players work in cooperation to defeat several hordes of computer-generated non-player monsters, trolls, goblins, and dragons of the sort that grow aggravated as the group progresses through a pre-programmed set of puzzles and objectives. This mode is officially referred to as dungeons, and those who are successful are rewarded with exciting incentives such as loot as well as progression in the game's central narrative. Dungeons get their name not necessarily because they involve dark underground prison cells resembling actual historic medieval equivalents (though there are dungeons of this sort in the game), but rather because the player content in this mode builds upon elements of chance and skill that were pioneered and developed in other popular and historic titles, including *World of Warcraft*, *Final Fantasy*, and *Everquest*.

Yinfay's viewers in the live chat had been discussing the subject of dungeons for days prior. There was some debate and uncertainty about how committed the developers of *Guild Wars 2* were to the dungeon mode, raising doubts regarding the prospect of receiving any new upcoming content:

May 30 17:32:27 <arthyria>	oh yin, will there be new dungeons?
May 30 17:32:35 <belphegordemon>	no
May 30 17:32:47 <belphegordemon>	they cancelled the dungeon team
May 30 17:32:56 <belphegordemon>	im so sad
May 30 17:33:04 <itiarathon>	We don't know if there are any new dungeons.

A prevalent topic, and one that arose quite frequently on Yinfay's stream despite her core focus being on sPvP, was to query the outlook for dungeons development. There were promises made by the game's developers, who assured that additional free-to-play content would be released at frequent intervals post-purchase of the core game. *Guild Wars 2* was intended to be a "living world" as the developers phrased it, and vitally this included extensions to all game modes.[12] Although the question in chat was intended for Yinfay, a few viewers on this occasion took it upon themselves to answer and discuss further on their own. One viewer, called Belphegordemon, shared the fact that the game publisher had already announced the cancellation of plans for future development on dungeons. The team, he pointed out, had disbanded to move on to other, more fruitful projects. A second viewer, Itiarathon, countered this position and challenged that "we don't know", later sharing further details and pointing out that there have been changes in the past countermanding official statements. In all, it was clear that viewers on Yinfay's stream cared about the preservation of many game modes, not only sPvP. They held out hope that at least there could be some possibility for future interest in dungeons.

This brief exchange is a small example of the many layers of expertise and the complexity that video game discussions can take on Twitch—yet another frame in the analysis. It is also indicative of the varied interests that can develop amongst viewers, even for those who routinely visit Yinfay's stream and who form a part of her relatively small community. Dungeons, to reiterate, were not a central component of Yinfay's routine broadcast, yet the occasional focus on dungeons in her chat showcases an ability that I have often observed in other streams across the platform. Gamers on Twitch sustain capacity as well as show an appetite for multiple concerns, divergent and sometimes intersecting lines of conversation.

Yinfay had seen Dungeons on the rise as a recent topic of interest amongst her viewers. She decided that she would run a few of them together live on stream with a select, lucky, few of her followers. This was to be her final day before departing on vacation, and she felt the need to interact more than usual and to make up for such an extended period of time away. Today, dungeons –not sPvP-would be Yinfay's preferred mode.

Having created a number of different accounts on both the EU and North American servers, Yinfay planned to include as many of her followers as possible in both regions by drawing teammates from her live chat. These were gamers who resided around the world, not only in Europe near Belgium where Yinfay herself physically lived. Yinfay sought to contact as many of her viewers as possible. She did not always invite others to play together, but this event was a special farewell. Yinfay would later explain to me in an interview that going ten days offline—even for an annual holiday—is harmful on Twitch not only since viewers experience it as a near

78 Not a Game

eternity away, leading to declines in followers, but also because long absences would negatively impact upon her chances to finally acquire a partnership deal with Twitch, the unspoken rule for which demands a critical mass of viewers as well as uninterrupted live streaming consistency.

Towards the end of my observations for the day, as a final bonus to maintain her holding power over the community before her departure, we were treated to one final out-of-the-ordinary surprise when Yinfay announced that in addition to the chance to play dungeons, she planned to hold a raffle for viewers to receive a postcard from her holiday destination:

May 31 14:58:20 <Yinfay *VOICE COMMENT*>	I will be back on the 10th. I will be back streaming. While I'm gone, I will do something exciting. Guys, I am going to send post cards to one…well not one… I'm going to see as many as I can send, but if you want the chance of getting a post card written by me, there we go! This is the command for it:
May 31 14:58:35 <Yinfay>	! postcard
May 31 14:58:47 <*lordnoodlebot>	Yin is going on vacation in June. So No stream for a week. I will miss you guys! But do you want the chance of a personal postcard? Click: www.tinyurl.com

On Twitch, it is common for streamers to make use of bots that can respond to chat commands for a variety of purposes. Yinfay's bot, named "lordnoodlebot", was useful in this case to help with relaying information about the upcoming hiatus from streaming and to link viewers to a public raffle website to draw for the chance to receive a physical postcard.

Trouble at Home

Things are far from utopian on any given live stream. After returning from her holiday, there were a few exchanges in Yinfay's live chat, upsetting the normal balance and tone of her live stream:

Jun 14 13:41:42 <charzooka>	Please delete your game!
Jun 14 13:41:43 <widdin>	GW2 [Guild Wars 2], biggest flop evva/facepalm
Jun 14 13:41:57 <fahimer>	oh lol i see
Jun 14 13:42:22 <sfpanzer *MODERTOR*>	please behave, Charzooka, and Widdin or I need to time you guys out
Jun 14 13:42:43 <widdin>	How is that not behaving? Lol
Jun 14 13:42:51 <widdin>	Just saying my own thoughts

Jun 14 13:42:53 <sfpanzer *MODERATOR*>	I'm just reminding you
Jun 14 13:43:05 <widdin>	I don't need any reminder but thanks anyways

Several viewers with whom I was not familiar as regular attendees appeared both agitated and aggressive. One viewer, named Charzooka, requested rather brazenly of Yinfay, "Please delete your game!" Another user called Widdin commented next in a mocking manner; "GW2 [Guild Wars 2], biggest flop evva/facepalm". As already established, Yinfay's channel is primarily dedicated to *Guild Wars 2*. This was a game that earned a place in a rather small group of video game titles to hit the top of the popularity charts. It certainly was not—as Widdin suggests—the "biggest flop", nor a failure of any kind. Nevertheless, there were far more recognizable games with much higher notoriety on Twitch, such as *League of Legends* or *Fortnite*. Perhaps these newcomers to the stream were fans of those other games, and this was the source of their malcontent.

I would soon learn the actual cause of this upset. As it happens, ArenaNet chose to host Yinfay's stream after she returned from holiday to give her channel a boost and to bring more attention to the game. In addition, they arranged with Twitch to have the stream broadcast on the home page of the website, bringing forth an even bigger flood of new visitors, as was the intended outcome. Unfortunately, what was not intended was to bring in a band of viewers such as these agitators, who were outsiders of the core community and who proved to be a rogue element on stream. The viewer Widdin is seen almost to campaign against Yinfay and her efforts to live stream *Guild Wars 2*, expounding his criticisms in toxic and wilful defiance. A few older and regular viewers are seen subsequently trying to defend their favourite game, and more importantly to preserve the integrity of their community, Yinfay's "home:"

Jun 14 13:44:27 <widdin>	Played Guild Wars 1; Guild Wars 2 was so overhyped
Jun 14 13:44:31 <xolsanctum>	Oh god…
Jun 14 13:44:50 <xolsanctum>	<_>
Jun 14 13:44:58 <sfpanzer *MODERTOR*>	it's a complete different game except for lore, @Widdin. Can't compare it
Jun 14 13:45:10 <kevinjakevin>	So long ago I played guild wars 2: O
Jun 14 13:45:38 <xolsanctum>	This is how to live in the past (Y)
Jun 14 13:45:43 <sfpanzer *MODERTOR*>	^This
Jun 14 13:45:50 <Yinfay *VOICE COMMENT*>	**Guys, be nice.**

Jun 14 13:45:49 <widdin>	I'm nice? Lol, no.
Jun 14 13:46:35 <patje1212>	being nice to viewers, I can live with that, but to mods is another question
Jun 14 13:46:48 <widdin>	Just because you were hosted by the GW2-official channel
Jun 14 13:46:54 <xolsanctum>	Nothing is wrong with mods
Jun 14 13:46:57 <xolsanctum>	O_o
Jun 14 13:47:12 <unknowninvader>	That changes everything, being hosted by GW2
Jun 14 13:47:16 <xolsanctum>	^This

This is clearly a frenzied exchange, the crux of which is to criticize *Guild Wars 2* for not being a worthy sequel to the first instalment in the franchise. Yinfay attempts to bring order to chat by pleading somewhat anxiously, "Guys, be nice". We can see a moderator in chat attempting to preserve the peace. Moderator Sfpanzor tries to both contain and respond to Widdin, proclaiming just how *Guild Wars 2* is a completely different game as compared to its predecessor. Adding to the drama, others in chat respond, some acknowledging that this disturbance is a result of having been hosted by ArenaNet.

Steadfast in her commitment to be as welcoming as possible on stream even as she finds her stream, under attack, Yinfay engages directly with her most vocal critic. Others in chat, including the moderator, also join in the conversation, attempting to debate the "meta" of *Guildwars 2*, which is to say the structure and game mechanics in comparison to different games within the same genre:

Jun 14 13:47:20 <Yinfay *VOICE COMMENT* >	Why do you not like the game Widdin? Why do you dislike it so much?
Jun 14 13:47:31 <widdin>	First of all its the questing, same thing over and over the WHOLE time until you're max.
Jun 14 13:47:40 <Yinfay *VOICE COMMENT* >	Oh…That's why. I see. But you still follow the Guild Wars 2 official channel? OK, let's compare it to another MMO … Here, in Guild Wars 2, only like maybe the first two minutes you have a complicated story, but after that you can go anywhere and whichever zone that you prefer. I am never obligated. I can go immediately to PvP and I am level 80 armor and 80 stats. Not a single other game, like MMO. has that. A lot of other MMOs force you to grind so much to actually participate. Also, you can get the best gear for free. You don't have to grind for pretty skins… You don't have to feel that in Guild Wars 2.

Jun 14 13:47:44 <widdin>	Pvp = Everyone has the same abilities (same for pve) b0ring
Jun 14 13:48:02 <deanarius>	lol wut?
Jun 14 13:48:10 <xolsanctum>	logic/10. Hates gw2 and thinks its overhyped. Still follows official gw2 channel. *insert meme*
Jun 14 13:48:16 <sfpanzer *MODERTOR*>	first of all that's not even true, Widdin
Jun 14 13:48:33 <xolsanctum>	Kappa
Jun 14 13:48:54 <widdin>	Been there, done that, 100% true sfPanzer
Jun 14 13:49:31 <sfpanzer *MODERTOR*>	and balancing is pretty hard so everyone having the same stuff is boring but that's just how it works in the end. You don't have to follow the meta builds, you can use whatever you want. I'm using stuff nobody else does and still win most of my games

"Oh … that's why", Yinfay remarks as if to empathize with Widdin and convey the sense that she understands his preference for different games. She explicates her position in more detail: "OK, let's compare it to another MMO … Here, in *Guild Wars 2*, only like maybe the first two minutes you have a complicated story, but after that you can go anywhere and whichever zone that you prefer. I am never obligated". A number of different themes come up in this conversation about the finer details of the metagame, but what is most apparent are the lengths to which the community was willing to defend their game and support their streamer. On several occasions at this point, and clearly in response to the building agitation, many challenged why Widden or any other negative viewers should be so persistent in debating the faults of *Guildwars 2* on a live stream that was so obviously setup and dedicated to celebrating its strengths. Tensions ran high as the heated discussion came to an end. Some viewers, including Yinfay herself, called for a change in topic. "Let's agree to disagree", suggested one viewer as a final solution. Just as soon as it surfaced, the trouble at home was thereafter concluded.

Conclusion: Not a Game

One might rightly ponder how it is that for a chapter titled "Not a Game" I should spend so much of it describing what are clearly detailed game play elements. Indeed, studying user activity on Twitch is akin to much earlier projects, which aim to conceptualize virtual communities and explore

82 Not a Game

"being digital".[13] Work of this kind is also aligned with a more recent turn in video games studies, which looks at intersections of gaming with material play settings in an attempt to overcome sharp conceptual divides that persist as a result of theories about the magic circle.[14] This chapter intends to argue that the gamer and the game are not separate aspects of game playing; rather, they are inextricably linked, but this is not to preclude the development of significant human contacts and the establishment of communities that go beyond the virtual world. We have inherited an understanding of gamers as "disaffected" and their gaming "habits" as a retreat from a world apparently deprived of hope and devoid of human relations. In the early days, some saw virtual worlds as a space for a brief reprieve, perhaps "cozy little worlds" within which one could positively develop a "second self" and a means to build identity and community.[15] More recently, however, others have found reason to be critical of entering "states of play" and "games of empire" that challenge how to live ethically in a time where reality is part digital, part social, part open, and part corporate.[16] The daily life of a gamer may still be usefully framed as an exploration of a "life world" dissolving boundaries between the real and unreal and offering a renewed sense of complete freedom of movement.[17] Notwithstanding this positive understanding of virtual worlds and their shaping of the individual gamer, gaming remains a point of contention and a source of serious misgivings as the video game industry continues to grow and gamers are spending more money and more time than ever before. That said, it is time to explore the potential of gaming as it now manifests on live streams, taking us beyond the prescribed limits of a digital world. It was not chiefly virtual worlds nor disaffection that I witnessed on my daily visits to the field on Twitch. Rather, the exchanges I saw were overwhelmingly intended to establish understanding, kinship, and, most importantly, caring for each fellow gamer, even in times of heated conflict.

In order to responsibly confront a dominant discourse that positions video gaming and gamers as socially and morally objectionable, it is important to emphasize from the very start that live streaming on Twitch is not a game. The most compelling aspect of T. L. Taylor's book *Play Between Worlds: Exploring Online Game Culture* is the notion that game worlds, especially those that are characterized by persistent open worlds populated by massive groups of players such as *Guildwars 2* or *World of Warcraft*, are indeed "life worlds" where sociality consists of, and is supported by, video game mechanics, yet importantly also interconnects with offline fan faire, reputation, responsibility, and dissolving boundaries of practices between worlds.[18] This suggests that while video games are indeed a focal point for gamers and gaming culture, video game play extends to many "in between" spaces that are co-constructed to interact with and sustain a community surrounding online games. Twitch, one might easily conclude, is a live video streaming website that offers a highly popular "in between world" where gamers are building communities much as enthusiasts have been doing since the dawn of home computers and the early internet—read here the aforementioned works of Rheingold. Once we focus on exploring the nature of streaming as an activity and not as a game, we can render what occurs during the community-building process and begin to understand why gamers choose to share this space; perhaps more importantly, we can understand what values they establish together and what agency they find on the platform.

Yet, as I suggest from my opening vignette, Twitch indicates how a focus, even on the game as interconnected or "in-between" space, falls short of a more complete analytic picture. How dissatisfied we were only to know the slim details about the avatar picture in question. As gamers on Twitch, many of us truly would like to know more about the people behind the story, the people behind the stream controlling all those avatars we see adventuring and battling each other in games. It is the pursuit of this sort of knowledge that makes an inquiry into virtual communities worthy of study because virtual communities are real communities consisting of real people and their real interests, a significant social element that we might better explore by deploying a frame analysis.

This chapter focuses on the example of Yinfay. She was explicit and insisted from the start that her mission was to cultivate a home for her viewers on Twitch. Many of the distinctions between what is real and what is virtual were seen to dissolve in the moment when Yinfay revealed to her community that she would be going on holiday. Indeed, she found herself in tension, but this was not something inherent to existential pulls or gaps between online and offline. Instead, it was temporal in origin. Yinfay was upset to be leaving her community for so long, and she felt a responsibility for that time and for those people who had grown accustomed to her presence on stream. It is not curious in the slightest that one would want to send physical postcards to virtual friends. Neither side had ever physically met, yet making that close material connection came naturally and easily.

Importantly, however, not all gamers on stream are alike, and there was certainly nothing overly utopic about this community. Yinfay found herself returning from a holiday to be confronted by a band of adversaries on stream. On Twitch, community is about making connections, and this is achieved in powerful ways by leveraging the technology of live video, including chat. This technical affordance does not, however, negate moments of disconnect nor protect entirely from disruptive people who aim primarily to sow discord. Yinfay, her moderators, and other loyal followers of the stream did what anyone in a conventional community would do when

84 Not a Game

they find themselves under threat and attack. They defended their game, but more importantly, they defended their stream—their "home"—and their values of care and consideration towards each other.

QUESTIONS

1. What is a "virtual community" and where do you see these forming?
2. Does a frame analysis help us better understand contemporary multi-player gaming? If so, how is this theory stronger than a theory of magic circles?
3. What holds streaming communities together, and what pulls them apart? When can a live video stream be considered a metaphorical "home"?

Notes

1 A Petrov's Defense is a common chess strategy where each opponent opens with a mirror move of each other effectively prolonging the initial standoff of a chess game.

2 A tonic in Guild Wars 2 is a special permanent potion that a player can drink in order to transform into a completely new avatar adorned with stylized armor pieces.

3 H. Rheingold, The Virtual Community: Homesteading on the Electronic Frontier (Boston, MA: Addison-Wesley, 1993), 6.

4 Bowman, Robert L.(1998) "Life on the electronic frontier: The application of technology to group work," The Journal for Specialists in Group Work, 23:4, 428–445.

5 While Howard Rheingold's The Virtual Community has been influential in shaping the discourse on online communities, several scholars have expressed critical perspectives on his work. Some of the notable critics include: S. Turkle, Life on the Screen: Identity in the Age of the Internet (New York: Simon & Schuster, 1995); M. Poster, "Cyberdemocracy: Internet and the Public Sphere," in Cyberdemocracy: Technology, Cities, and Civic Networks, (London: Routledge, 1995), 201–17; V. Mosco, The Digital Sublime: Myth, Power, and Cyberspace (Cambridge, MA: MIT Press, 2004). See also, for more recent critiques, J. Bridle, New Dark Age: Technology and the End of the Future (London: Verso Books, 2018); S. Bardzell, "Feminist HCI: Taking Stock and Outlining an Agenda for Design," Proceedings of the SIGCHI Conference on Human Factors in Computing Systems, 2010, 1301–10.

6 Rheingold, H. (1993). The virtual community: Homesteading on the electronic frontier. The MIT press URL: http://www.rheingold.com/vc/book/1.html; introduction.

7 Even if we adjust for Rheingold's time of writing when the technology of the internet was completely nascent in the early 1990s, there is reason to argue that his viewpoints are overly optimistic. See for example: Ester, P. and Vinken, H. 2003. "Debating civil society: on the fear for civic decline and hope for

the Internet alternative". International Sociology, 18(4): 659–680; Feenberg, A. and Bakardjieva, M. (2004). "Virtual community: no 'killer application'". New Media & Society, 6(1): 37–43; and Dahlberg, L. 2007. "Rethinking the fragmentation of the Cyberpublic: from consensus to contestation". New Media & Society, 9(5): 827–847.

8 See: Negroponte, Nicholas (1995). Being Digital. Hodder and Stoughton: Great Britain, and Turkle, S. (1995). Life on the Screen: Identity in the Age of the Internet. Simon & Schuster Paperbacks: New York.

9 Glas, R. Kristine Jorgensen, Torill Mortensen and Luca Rossi (2011). "Framing the game: four game-related approaches to Goffman's frames" in Online Gaming in Context: The Social and Cultural Significance of Online Games. Eds Crawford G., Victoria K. Gosling and Ben Light. Routledge. Goffman's 'social frame theory,' in Goffman, E. (1974) Frame Analysis: An Essay on the Organization of Experience, New York, Harper and Row.

10 Glas, R. et al. "Framing the game"; 141.

11 Goffman, E. (1974). "Frame analysis"; 45.

12 Arena Net (2013). Living World in Guild Wars 2. Accessed 8/31/2018 URL: https://www.guildwars2.com/en/news/living-world-in-guild-wars-2/

13 Ibid. Negroponte, Nicholas (1995). "Being Digital"; and Turkle, S. (1995). "Life on the Screen"

14 Taylor, N. Jennifer Jenson, Suzanne Castell, Barry Dilouya (2014). "Public Displays of Play: Studying Online Games in Physical Settings". in Journal of Computer-Mediated Communication 19 (2014) 763–779.

15 Rheingold, H. (1993). The virtual community: Homesteading on the electronic frontier. The MIT press URL: http://www.rheingold.com/vc/book/1.html (Introduction); Turkle, S. (1984). The Second Self: Computer and the human spirit. The MIT Press edition (2005).

16 Balkin, J. M., & Noveck, B. S. (2006). State of Play: Law, Games, and Virtual Worlds (Ex Machina: Law, Technology, and Society). NYU Press; and Dyer-Witheford N., & Peuter G. (2009). Games of Empire: Global Capitalism and Video Games. Minneapolis: University of Minnesota Press.

17 Jenkins, H (1998). From Barbie to Mortal Kombat: Gender and Computer Games. Cambridge, Massachusetts: The MIT Press; and Taylor T.L. (2006) Play Between Worlds: Exploring Online Game Culture. The MIT Press.

18 Ibid. Taylor (2006) "Play Between Worlds".

4

LUDIC DIVIDES

Introduction

In *Zap: The Rise and Fall of ATARI* (1984), Scott Cohen tells the story of "7 princes" and their rise to power, from undergraduate students and hobby tinkerers to the founders and upper management of ATARI incorporated. The beginning epigraph in this historical account offers a striking point of reference that highlights the scope of the early gaming industry as well as the corporate empire owned and operated by these first gamers. Cohen recalls the total amount requested for aid to all of Central America in 1984 as 600 million USD; that was less than one-tenth of what Americans would spend that year on coin-operated video games operated by ATARI.[1] Nearly a decade later, in *Game Over: How Nintendo Zapped an American Industry, Captured Your Dollars, and Enslaved Your Children* (1993), David Sheff recounts a similar tale, only this time the princes would be "samurai otaku", computer "geek enthusiasts" of the highest order hailing from Japan. Nintendo had become a corporate force that could not be ignored. In the early 1990s, the company netted as much as all the American movie studios and profited more than the three American television networks combined (ABC, CBS, and NBC).[2] These stories are the end result of a process that would become increasingly prominent throughout video game history—the "zap"—which mobilizes players themselves, rendering their "immaterial labour" and their ludic space, a space of spontaneous and undirected playfulness, into tangible and massive capital gains. Behind each commercial success there lies a "workers' history of videogaming", perhaps best described in terms of its underlying

DOI: 10.4324/9781003341079-5

neoliberal logic as a "specter of entrepreneurship" blurring the boundaries between work and leisure and maintaining, as some have suggested, an ever-expanding "playbor force".[3]

This chapter traces a similar process to "the zap" exploring in contemporary times what I call a "ludic divide".[4] Gamers on Twitch are now negotiating new challenges in going corporate. They find their streaming communities under heavy strain, culminating in an ultimate pressure to convert their once untapped ludic pleasure and to trade in their playful purpose to directly benefit large-scale profitability as well as charitable causes. The chapter is an ethnographic account of the live streamers who call themselves "speedrunners" and who play the classic video game *Super Mario 64*. Among other contributions, the chapter offers an account of how a gamer persona, a persona that ostensibly must appear unconcerned with a wider world beyond the virtual, remains foremost dedicated to other fellow gamers and in service to loyal followers and subscribers. The chapter details, as elsewhere in this book, how gamer subjects develop a notion of self that is fundamentally located in the community. I add to this notion the premise that streaming communities must also be considered communities of work. Streamers and viewers are understood as sharing in the co-labor that produces and sustains live streams through hard times.

Corporate Infiltrations

It was not my primary objective during fieldwork to pursue any opportunities to speak with the management, employees, or partners involved in the technical backend of Twitch. I did not go out of my way to seek out staff or to spend much time inquiring about those responsible for maintaining or adding new functionality to the platform, for the reason that mapping those technical aspects would invite a counterproductive overemphasis on the technology of streaming itself rather than on the people who form an inexorable part of its social structure. My participants, furthermore, were not usually in close connection with Twitch administrators or web designers either; consequently, I doubted that contact with anyone from that side of the business could reveal much about the actual engagement, values, or practices on the live streams that I was interested in exploring day-to-day. By my estimation, there would be precious little opportunity to gather auxiliary data or to learn about the associations and mechanisms that drive one of the world's busiest and most successful live streaming services. Yet when one opportunity did arise, I set my scepticism aside. A Twitch developer was attending an undergraduate class taught by a colleague of mine and was eager to discuss her work with me when she learned about my book project. This was an offer I could not refuse.

88 Ludic divides

Annie (a pseudonym) was a co-founder and CEO for a company providing Twitch with technical and web development services on several internal functions for streaming. Speaking to me on the condition that her name and company would remain anonymous, she reflected on her personal role and commented as a provider within a larger community of developers. She was one of many thousands involved in the planning, coding, and presentation of core and auxiliary features on Twitch, and her company was only one of dozens harboring ambitions to win larger contracts and drive more engagement on the platform.

To be specific, at the time of our meeting, Annie was directly involved with extending features to the live chat functionality on Twitch. Her knowledge of upcoming changes to these streaming functions gave me an invaluable opportunity to glean some of the unexpected design decisions and goals occurring behind the scenes in response to evolving needs from streamers, viewers, and other stakeholders. All parties involved in streaming seemed to wish for more effective feature mechanisms and to communicate better on the platform. Further, there were many sponsors on Twitch—especially brands dealing in gaming supplies and peripheral equipment—who desired to capture more attention and perhaps find new ways of generating supplementary income through driving sales in their online stores.

Annie revealed firstly and above all else a very sobering fact, one that perhaps should not have come as a surprise when considering the ongoing growth and speculation on Twitch: she claimed with utmost honesty that most developers for Twitch—in her experience—were primarily and often solely motivated by acquiring fast capital gains. They were excited by the profit that they might derive from gamer's activities on the website; even more nefarious, they were not necessarily motivated by any intimate knowledge of gaming or inspired by any passion for streaming. They often had no expertise about video games whatsoever, and most surprisingly, they revealed limited experience even for running a web-based development business. To be clear, when it comes to corporations, profits are expected to be of paramount importance, but according to Annie, even developers working for these Twitch auxiliaries often initiated their contracts having only the slightest experience interacting with gamers or game developers. Speaking this time for herself, Annie clarified that in the beginning, she and her colleagues viewed the gaming phenomenon on Twitch simply as an untapped resource:

> The story of our company is actually quite odd. Myself and John are the founders. We met doing a program called the Next 36, which is a program for students or recent graduates who have an interest in

entrepreneurship. [The program is for people who] have no experience with putting together teams and it gives a bit of money as well as course material. So, we took courses over the summer in entrepreneurship and how to run a company and so we started last year at this time. We met at this event, and we immediately liked each other. We were like, okay well that is cool. We kind of want to start a business but we didn't really know what we were going to do. I heard a few things about Esports in the news and was like we should definitely do something with Esports. There is a lot of potential here. It is totally untapped. So, we just dove into it.

To be fair, not everyone who arrives on Twitch arrives with much of a "game plan". I, myself, arrived without much of an understanding or expectation about what sorts of activities I would get involved with on the website. Yet, to my surprise, this was a similar experience for Annie, the founder and CEO of a software company seeking, from the start, to work as a Twitch partner. Annie had assembled her company with little more than the impetus to build on a school project, to capitalize on a trend that she had read about while perusing the news.

Somewhat disbelieving, I pressed further to inquire whether perhaps Annie herself had at least had some experience with playing video games at any point in her life. She responded:

I played games as a kid but hadn't really been following games in recent years. Same with my partner. My parents say that I was playing video games when I was four-years-old on our home computer, but it was something I kind of fell out of. I guess just my friend group and circle of friends weren't really playing games. But I still followed them **because I had boyfriends** and stuff. I was not really aware of the phenomenon going on Twitch, so we dove into it. We figured there is something we can do there. At the beginning we thought we could be a '**give away platform.**' We saw people doing 'give-aways' on Twitch and we said we could make this a lot easier. We could make this more streamlined. We also saw it as a way to bring in brands. Because we knew at some point we would have to make money from our endeavour. We thought that if brands want to advertise on Twitch, then they could do that through our give away platform and then we could give away like free cans of Red Bull **or whatever** (my emphasis added).

What people say about their activities and habits online versus what they do is, in truth, oftentimes incongruent. Whilst Annie claimed not to be a gamer herself and supported this position with the relevant testimony

90 Ludic divides

from her parents, she was able to offer several examples of gameplay that indicated a much more informed and longstanding relationship throughout her life. Following old boyfriends and refining her business senses were the official bylines of our initial talk, but Annie had in fact, on several occasions, at least trialed playing video games; moreover, now that she had developed her company, she understood quite well how to read what was relevant and current in modern games. The fact remains, however, that Annie had exhibited no interest in Twitch prior to her business venture and ostensibly invested even less into video games before arriving at her current position.

After describing her background to me, Annie went on to discuss what her company eventually found lacking on Twitch and thus identified the strategic gap that she and her partners would fill in the development market space. They began by building code to better enable "give-aways" for viewers. A give-away on the platform is understood precisely as its name implies—that is, for streamers or game studios to distribute prizes for viewers, usually at random, but also sometimes attached to competitions including raffles and trivia contests. These incentives are designed to reward sustained viewership. Streamers often wish to give back to their viewers as well as work towards financially supporting their own ability to carry on streaming on regular schedules over the long term. The design challenge, as Annie saw it, was to learn how to accomplish give-aways without disrupting the normal content of a given broadcast, without overwhelming or aggravating the viewer base, who may consider the practice as a form of unsolicited offer.[5] Annie's solution was to attach a give-away website with automated bot functionality integrated directly into the Twitch chat.

Unfortunately for Annie, her company's initial efforts to launch a give-away feature for Twitch met with, in her own words, "abysmal failure". Since her company's final design was to drive users off Twitch and onto a separate and distinct website to facilitate the distribution of give-away prizes, streamers and viewers both claimed during trials of the feature that they wanted to retain traffic on their own live streams and not drive people away. What is more, they did not see a need to automate or streamline the give-away process, which they had always self-managed and personally controlled in the past. I was not surprised in the slightest to find that the "or whatever" attitude developed fruitless results for Annie's corporate infiltration. The give-away feature was promptly rejected by gamers on Twitch, and it would prove insufficient for Annie and her partner, as software developers, to simply "dive in" for profit. Annie informed me that her team ultimately shifted their focus to servicing only much larger Twitch events where organizational requirements could be better understood and partnerships with prize companies (as well as profit sharing) could be more easily defined.

ACTIVITY 1

Take a moment to consider a few online social media applications that have emerged in recent years. How have these "apps" evolved to include monetization for driving corporate profit? Are these monetization schemes helpful to the communities that use those apps? Which apps accomplish monetization best?

Hard Work

Jun 25 12:28:40 <ssbdennis>	the streaming world seems to be hard
Jun 25 12:30:16 <abeltabel>	it's almost like a company
Jun 25 12:30:16 <Liveegg *VOICE COMMENT* >	Dude, streaming is hard…You can do it through hard work, but you have to work your ass off pretty much. There is no easy ride to be a successful streamer. You either have to be really fucking good at a video game—like the best in the world—or you have to dedicate your whole life to streaming. You have to stream every day for a huge amount of time…

As the brief exchange above suggests, streaming on Twitch is hard work. If not like running a company, then it is clearly something into which gamers must invest a significant amount of time before they achieve any considerable following. Most visitors (viewers, not streamers) may set out to immediately have fun, to connect with others, or to share a love of video games. They may find opportunities to meet other likeminded people; they may even develop long-lasting relationships that extend later into connections offline, but the job of building long-lasting communities in which this kind of sociality is enabled to flourish is indeed very hard work for those who create and maintain their channels.

Curiously, not many streamers that I followed and with whom I would eventually partner on this book were altogether forthcoming about the parameters of their work. The few insights that they were willing to share

92 Ludic divides

during my years spent in the field usually came in the form of very short acumens on how wonderful an opportunity stream was or about how exciting it was to finally gain recognition and acceptance for playing their video games. Occasionally, a few did share how tired they felt after streaming for such long hours near the end of a busy week or how they looked forward to a well-deserved vacation and some time off after playing a particularly "grindy" video game, but it seemed that the sort of discussion that would expose the business side of streaming was not a topic easily open for discussion. It was especially taboo to bring up streaming as any form of work in the larger, more populated streams, as if to acknowledge such a thing on camera was to be disruptive to the overall immersive experience. Gamers on Twitch were ostensibly more interested in preserving their own fantasies about gaming and a carefree streamer life. They apparently visited Twitch to live vicariously and crucially, perhaps, to find peace in an environment premised upon lifting the pressures of everyday life

The finer affective qualities of streaming in terms of working hard, however, were a reoccurring subject of concern for one outlier streamer and partner of mine called Liveegg. Liveegg was the sole streamer among dozens contributing to this book who frequently proved quite receptive to meta-level talk about his work in streaming. In addition to his own viewpoints, he often counselled other streamers who were actively trying to earn a supplementary income in his streaming category.

On July 1st, 2015, while I was halfway through my participant observation for the day, a few viewers revealed their appreciation as well as admiration for the work that was clearly beginning to show positive gains for Liveegg:

Jul 1 11:44:35 <SouringWombat>	you're pretty good at this Mario thing
Jul 1 11:45:36 <Aragog127>	Egg I gotta say it's impressive how much you've improved since I started watching. You keep shaving minutes off every couple months …
Jul 1 11:45:39 <Aragog127>	Keep up the great work
Jul 1 11:45:40 <SouringWombat>	Yeah congrats on the 1:41
Jul 1 11:45:45 <Yashimisu>	I had this game on ds
Jul 1 11:45:50 <Yashimisu>	beat the game
Jul 1 11:46:00 <Aragog127>	Well I've watched since he was working on beating 1:49

SouringWombat, a regular viewer and subscriber to the channel, commented first with a somewhat smug brashness—"your pretty good at this Mario thing"—as is indicated by his later use of the kappa emote but also revealed through his familiar tactic of prompting a discussion via a short, punchy, and timely comment. Liveegg was a streamer dedicated exclusively to the "speedrunning" of *Super Mario 64*, one of the many Nintendo classics that features prominently on Twitch. Speedrunning is the practice of attempting to complete a series of video game objectives as quickly as possible, submitting times in a competition against other gamers in the community, each with the aspiration to achieve the world record for fastest run. Liveegg and others to be discussed through this chapter were speedrunners committed entirely to *Super Mario 64*, their channels dedicated to sharing their world record attempts as well as practice each day. These speedrunners often showed significant developments in their proficiency over time as they trained for several months on end.[6] Another viewer, Aragog127, commented next on Liveegg's stream: "Egg I gotta say it's impressive how much you've improved since I started watching. You keep shaving minutes off every couple months ..." This viewer got closer to an important point (to which SouringWombat no doubt was alluding to prior)—this is a game where every second counts.

Super Mario 64 was published in 1996 for the Nintendo 64 game console. It was one of the earliest examples of what would ultimately mark an important historical shift and a sea change for the video game industry when games began moving towards real-time 3-D rendered content. What made *Super Mario 64* stand out and what has sustained it as a widely popular title is its unique fluidity that expands the gameplay across all three dimensions of virtual movement. The player is afforded an opportunity to achieve a very high skill cap in gameplay just by shifting the camera by a few micro inputs, and by consequence, no two speedruns ever play out quite the same. Players in the speedrunning community, despite this volatility in movement, aim for absolute consistency in their execution of controller inputs. Many speedrunners use the term "frame-perfect" to indicate their mastery over each rendered frame of their playthrough when analysing their runs.

Liveegg went to great lengths to develop a visual fidelity to his stream and to communicate the details of his goals to his viewers. His stream appears tidy and organized when compared to most others on Twitch, even in relation to other runners within the same *Super Mario 64* category. Not a pixel of space is wasted, and no superfluous data is communicated that might diverge from a complete focus on his world record attempts. On the right-hand side, taking up easily two-thirds of the image, appeared the gameplay itself. Here, we can see various meta-data from the game, such as how many stars have been obtained, the current in-game time counter, and the number of secondary objectives, such as total coins collected. To the

94 Ludic divides

FIGURE 4.1 Liveegg's Twitch Scene.

left, there is an application widget designed to track Liveegg's run. In this widget, there appears a list of "splits" from the game, with time stamps fitting neatly together and correlating to each section of the speedrun. Large green numbers also keep track of how long the run has been ongoing, while in smaller white numbers, we can see the live updated times of each section already completed as well as those coming up next (Figure 4.1)

The plethora of data available on Liveegg's streams enables veteran viewers to understand at each moment how well things are progressing, as well as instances where Liveegg might need to save time.[7] Finally, in the bottom left of the video stream, there is a virtual representation of Liveegg's game controller. Here, viewers can observe in real time his actual button inputs and combinations, further illustrating the level of skill in his gameplay. Liveegg often justified to myself and to his viewers on stream how virtualizing his controller serves as a way to increase a sort of embodied empathy for his actions leading on from moment to moment. Many of us remembered and could re-live times from years past when we too wrestled intensely with our controllers. Liveegg worked intently to bring back this fading affective dimension of play.

Later in the broadcast and closer to the end of my observation for the day, another long-time viewer, AieXSM64, continued on the theme of working hard. This time, he moved the conversation to focus on his own circumstances of employment. This was an opportunity to glean something about how gamers often look to streamers on Twitch for guidance. It was a chance to see how leadership on the platform can also extend more explicitly into the realm of work, and not only in relation to video games. AieXSM64 looked to Liveegg, his favourite streamer and leader of the community, for advice about a job. He asked: "Egg should I do something that I don't like … e.g. if you don't like a job but keep doing it?" To which we see an unfolding of responses in the live chat:

Jul 1 11:58:35 <AieXSM64>	Egg should I do something that I don't like…e.g. if you don't like a job but keep doing it.
Liveegg <Broadcaster>:	**I don't know man. It depends what your other options are.**
Jul 1 11:59:55 <AieXSM64>	this job i do, i have been making good money for almost 3 weeks…
Jul 1 12:00:15 <AieXSM64>	but it's not what im gonna do in the future.
Liveegg <Broadcaster>:	**If you have a job that's paying good money. Just do it. Do that job, save up some money, and then once you feel like you have a plan figured out for the future, as soon as you feel like you have a plan figured out, I mean shit you want to do now and what you want to do in the future, then quit that job. But it's good to save up money. I wish I had money. I had a job, then I quit. And I regret quitting now.**

Liveegg's response, as was often the case when he was made to feel responsible for his viewers, was to be somewhat reticent. He deflected with a counterprobe of his own: "It depends". Asking for further clarification into the viewer's cryptic dilemma; Liveegg was ready to learn more. The viewer responded: "I have been making good money for almost 3 weeks, but it's not what I'm going to do in the future". As I observed this query unfolding in chat, my attention was split to also focus on the developing speedrun. I wondered how old this viewer was. Was this his first job? What were his duties exactly? Did anyone on the stream seriously consider three weeks to be a protracted length of time?

In a rare display of confidence and apparently not burdened by any of the questions I wanted to ask, Liveegg—still controlling Mario and carrying on his speedrun—swiftly answered, "If you have a job that's paying good money, just do it". He then continued with more clarification: "Do that job, save up some money and then once you feel like you have a plan figured out for the future, as soon as you feel like you have a plan figured out, and I mean shit you want to do now and what you want to do in the future, then quit that job". This response was in complete character

96 Ludic divides

for Liveegg, as I had grown to know him better over the years of streaming on Twitch. Liveegg had himself found a place on Twitch while in between jobs and after having left his university bachelor's degree with only a few courses remaining towards completion of his transcript. He had quit all pursuits to take up playing video games full-time, not because he saw streaming as a glamourous career or that he thought he would be one to make millions on the platform, but rather because he had found a pursuit in playing and streaming that he saw to be worthy of his time. Liveegg was admittedly unsure of what he wanted to do with his own life in the long term, yet he was absolutely resolved on this one position: happiness meant being capable of doing "shit you want to do" whatever that might in practice entail. Crucially, however, in choosing what he wanted to do, Liveegg revealed himself to be as dedicated, disciplined, and mindful as any world-class athlete might be, offering his viewers the inspiration of his own skills and achievements, mentorship, and a shared dedication to playing the game expertly.

This exchange continued. Liveegg offered some of his own recent experience in response to another commenter in chat. This time we learn more about Liveegg's views on higher education: "College ... I didn't think college sucked. I thought compared to high school, college was amazing". To which AieXSM64 replied, "As an experience yea ... but as for the future then what ... you get a paper that will get you an average job working for someone else." Finally, Liveegg concludes, "Ya dude, I'm not about that life either. That's why I'm on my ass right now playing video games. I just do what I want to do. That's life to me".

This exchange and Liveegg's final words might appear brash and a rather narrow adoption of the popular adage "do what you love", but it is indicative of a more telling inner predicament and sometimes as well a contradiction for gamers on live streams.[8] Gamers do not find themselves streaming alone. Alternatively put, they do not carry on the work of streaming in the long term for themselves individually; rather, they are active on the platform with significant others; they stream not for themselves but ultimately for the viewers. Though Liveegg claims to be merely doing what he wants to do and only for himself, he is clearly exhibiting through his actions on stream quite the contrary. He is serving others, and he is helping those in chat find their own way of working (hard) through life.

"Take Our Energy⌐ つ ●_● ⌐ つ": Viewership as Co-Labour

Liveegg's viewers demonstrated how the job of sustaining a live stream sometimes cannot be a solitary pursuit. Streaming can be the opposite of casual game-playing as viewers engage in a form of co-labour, which in turn propels the community forward through hard times. I observed one day how Liveegg was having a very difficult day:

Jun 23 10:52:20 <zykotiik>	Did he mess up and continue the run?
Jun 23 10:52:55 <skyru666>	yes
Jun 23 10:53:40 <ts03002215>	egguOgre
Jun 23 10:53:58 <Liveegg>	this is probably the most frustrated i can even remember being in my speedrunning career
Jun 23 10:54:05 <Liveegg>	today is seriously insane
Jun 23 10:54:13 <yoshistar95>	:\
Jun 23 10:54:13 <xmidnax>	what happened, i just came by: (
Jun 23 10:54:24 <womplord>	i like this new strat
Jun 23 10:54:28 <skyru666>	call on the powers of cthulu
Jun 23 10:54:31 <Liveegg>	i've been streaming for almost 3 hours and 30 mins and despite trying as hard as i can i simply cannot make it to basement

The user Zykotiik asks, after having only recently arrived on the stream, why Liveegg appeared to be in such a state of utter resignation: "Did he mess up and continue the run?" Meanwhile, the speedrun clock was still counting, yet Mario, who is normally seen leaping and flipping acrobatically through the air, stood still without any indication of input to the controller. "Yes", Skyru666 replied. Another, Ts03002215, remarked simply "EgguOgre" (this was a command line for a unique-to-Liveegg emoji resembling the ogre character Shrek from the Pixar animated film franchise of the same name). Paying subscribers to the channel form a special group that, by providing a nominal fee of $5 USD per month, retained the privilege of using EgguOgre as well as watching the live stream completely free of advertisements.[9]

Amid some puzzlement and mounting concern in chat, I also noticed the title for today's broadcast. It read as usual "120 Star Speedruns" to indicate how Liveegg was intending to complete the game, but it was edited this time to include the unusual subtitle "[100% focus, no mic]. Unlike on most other live-streams, Liveegg did not make use of a web camera during his streaming sessions—that space was already carefully reserved for his virtual controller—however today he took the added and extreme measure of muting his microphone, despite it being a much less dispensable component on any live stream. The microphone is the primary device serving as a facilitator for discussions. It is usually the main communicative bridge for the streamer to answer questions from chat while sustaining simultaneous

98 Ludic divides

live gameplay. I myself watched in puzzlement. Why had Liveegg elected to turn his mic off for the day?

The stream continued. Mario, who no longer stood still, appeared to be sitting down with his legs spread out as if to exhibit his own exhaustion and frustration in virtual form. "Imma tired", the in-game avatar exclaimed [read in a Mario voice] while sitting outstretched and yawning. *Super Mario 64* is programmed to be a high-speed and fast-paced video game, as already established, but the game's developers had foresight enough to include a line of code instructing Mario to sit down automatically when a lack of player control input is detected. Mario's movements appear now very lethargic on the screen, and his speech dialogue was filled with sighs and yawns.

The clock continued ticking forward. Liveegg, with his microphone still disengaged, decided nevertheless to respond to chat. He typed rather than spoke: "this is probably the most frustrated I can even remember being in my speedrunning career; Today is seriously insane". Now clearly alarmed, another new arrival asked, "what happened, I just came by ☺". Following this, the viewer Xmidnax replied rather flippantly, "I like this new strat" as if to suggest that leaving the controller alone and allowing Mario to rest was somehow going to improve the run. "I've been streaming for almost 3 hours and 30 mins and despite trying as hard as I can, I simply can't make it to basement", Liveegg clarified. The problem, as I surmised at this point, lay in an early section of the speedrun where Mario needed to gain access to the basement of the castle by gathering the first ten stars and subsequently locating a basement key. There are several time-saving strategies in this section of the game, plus a few of the most difficult-to-execute mechanical movements on the entire speedrun (needless to say, abandoning the controller was not part of the plan).

With all hope nearly gone the stream continued for a further minute without any movement input from Liveegg. Mario promptly fell asleep and now snored heavily (Figure 4.2).

The viewer TS03002215 was the first to break the "silence", this time showing serious support and evincing his long-time relationship to the channel: "Just don't mind it too much Egg. Remember those days when you were stuck in the lobby? Take a rest". To clarify, the lobby is the very first area inside the castle at the start of the game. To gain access to it, Mario must open a front door, thereby triggering a pre-rendered introduction video that sets the context for the game for new players. This establishes the imperilled-princess narrative as well as signals Mario's main objective to seek out all the world's power stars. The scene itself spans only ten seconds; however, speedrunners are able to skip the scene entirely, a

Ludic divides 99

FIGURE 4.2   Image of Mario sleeping during Liveegg's pause.

skip that they refer to as the "Lakitu Skip" after the Lakitu companion who appears as the messenger in the cut scene. Through clever use of game mechanics, players deploy a series of camera controls in combination with a number of flips, turns, and long jumps to bypass the door of the castle and arrive inside the lobby. This was a "strat" that Liveegg had spent weeks perfecting during his earliest days on stream. He understood then that losing even ten seconds would eliminate any chances of setting a world record time, and the viewer TS03002215 (who remembered that struggle) reminded Liveegg to persevere.

Perhaps a rest was in order. Yet another paying subscriber, Yoshistar95, added his own input to lighten the mood and offer a kind of relief to the distressed streamer. Yoshistar95 was well known on the stream for having created his own YouTube channel dedicated almost entirely to logging humorous moments from previous Liveegg broadcasts. To show his unique brand of support, Yoshistar95 linked everyone in the chat to a clip featuring another notoriously difficult area of the game called "Plunder in the Sunken Ship". Here, Liveegg is seen attempting to control Mario through an underwater shipwreck to recover one hundred lost coins. In the clip, a donation to Liveegg comes ringing through mid-run with an attached automatic voice message. The message is a joke, jeering at Liveegg for his enraged reactions during difficult splits. Liveegg is heard laughing

100 Ludic divides

hysterically in the clip. Now the viewer, Yoshistar95, tried to inspire Liveegg and make light of his present situation. Would Liveegg end the stream for the day and take a rest after the hard-fought runs or continue as his viewer implored him?

"Today is different from those days. This is on a different level. I'm used to playing like shit, saving and quitting etc. and still getting pb [personal best] pace runs multiple times per stream. I can play bad and pb, but I can't even get to basement right now. It's unexplainable", Liveegg continued to lament despite the best efforts of his most loyal viewer base. Still more of them erupted in support through the live chat:

Jun 23 10:55:38 <ihgkowz>	everyone has bad days and egg, tomorrow will be a new day punWaifu
Jun 23 10:55:43 <knowmadss>	practice bro
Jun 23 10:56:39 <snow_it_all>	you're doing great!
Jun 23 10:56:48 <womplord>	have you checked the door with the big lock?
Jun 23 10:56:50 <skyru666>	usually i use the powers of marijuana to get me through tough times
Jun 23 10:56:54 <xhoshikox>	Shut up yoshi
Jun 23 10:57:01 <xhoshikox>	Egg you can pb
Jun 23 10:57:02 <snow_it_all>	glory rises and falls, just keep on trying
Jun 23 10:57:20 <puncayshun>	plz talk to us egg
Jun 23 10:57:23 <puncayshun>	use mic
Jun 23 10:57:49 <ihgkowz>	I think the best thing you can do in this situation egg is practice, do a no reset just to do it, or keep trying! cirHappy
Jun 23 10:57:50 <xhoshikox>	Pls no bully, egg is having a rough night: (
Jun 23 10:58:08 <yoshistar95>	this will be it
Jun 23 10:58:09 <xmidnax>	Go egg FrankerZ go egg FrankerZ
Jun 23 10:58:11 <zykotiik>	Send him vibes
Jun 23 10:58:12 <ts03002215>	and i can say this will be it
Jun 23 10:58:28 <ihgkowz>	\punWaifu/take our energy!\punWaifu/
Jun 23 10:58:41 <xhoshikox>	\punWaifu/
Jun 23 10:59:10 <xmidnax>	\FrankerZ/take me\FrankerZ/

The Viewer Ihgkowz, who was not a subscriber to Liveegg's channel but nevertheless a subscriber to an affiliated Mario channel elsewhere, remarked: "everyone has bad days and egg, tomorrow will be a new day 'punWaifu'". This viewer used the "punWaifu" emoji, which was not one of Liveegg's channel designs but still encouraging. The emoji depicted an anime girl winking and wearing a Mario cap. Snow_it_all cheered next: "you're doing great!" Following shortly thereafter, Skyru666 jocularly shared his own advice: "usually I use the powers of marijuana to get me through tough times". Amidst this wave of support, I also noted that some viewers were disturbed by the lack of microphone communication. One viewer requested that it be turned back on, while another asked simply for Liveegg to return his focus and to continue practicing.

Towards the end of this moment of extensive communication, a familiar sight on Twitch was unveiled. When all else fails to motivate on stream, viewers often turn to their own best power of influence over any livestream—their sheer massive numbers. Unable to use voices of their own, they began to spam text messages as if stirring the crowd up in support for Liveegg. "Take our energy!", one viewer exclaimed. "Take me!", another copied. These viewers demonstrated their worth and their co-labor in chat. Their job for the day was to resuscitate the stream and inspire Liveegg onward. Soon after, Liveegg did continue his run. In fact, he returned to his world record attempts for another 2 hours and 10 minutes. Most importantly, he managed to overcome his feelings of resignation. He was finally able to conquer the castle basement.

ACTIVITY 2

This chapter considers community engagements as they correlate to co-labor on live streams. The blurring of work and play in streaming is also a near-constant feature on Twitch. Do you see work and play integrated into other settings? Where else might you see people coming together and sharing their labor for the sake of community online?

"Living the Dream" (Until Thirty)

On August 11th, 2015, a viewer named Bullofbashan enquired about the enigmatic screen name of a new streamer we were watching play *Super Mario 64*. The streamer, who was a colleague of Liveegg, replied, "Hey what's up, my name was originally SimplyN64. Soon everybody started calling me Simply, and then I got a name change. Back in the day, name changes were a thing, but they aren't anymore". In fact, speedrunning has historical ties that originated long before the advent of Twitch and even before the popularization of live streams in general, but Simply himself had only started to play as a competitive speedrunner shortly after the website had gone independent as a platform from its parent website Justin.tv, and before it was purchased by Amazon. As Twitch grew in popularity and profitability—after Simply joined—there were several new rules brought forth, notable among them the requirement for streamers to retain permanent names for their channels.[10]

Having only just arrived on Simply's stream a few weeks earlier, I, myself, was only just beginning to become familiar with this community. On that day, I began recording several important channel details, noticing, as usual, the title of the stream. Simply straightforwardly titled his business for the day "120 star speedruns, slowly walk up and pb/wr". I had watched hundreds of 120-star speedruns by this point, but I was nevertheless excited. Without offense to Liveegg or any of the others, this was a rare chance to observe not just anyone's speedrun—this was going to be one of Simply's famed attempts. I noted that the abbreviation "pb" [personal best] had been a common addendum to daily titles; however, seeing "wr" [world record] this time was not to be overlooked. We learned how Simply, who had already achieved several world records in the past, was attempting to reclaim the right to be called the fastest. For him, this was truly a realistic goal. He was already a Top 3 *Mario 64* speedrunner. There were two other categories for *Mario*, the 16-star and the 70-star runs, both much shorter in length yet each offering markedly different challenges to overcome. Simply was already the record holder for the 70-star variant, a version in which Mario only obtains the minimum necessary stars to arrive at the final boss. Besides this, he was also very nearly the best at 16-star, though he often admitted that he did not enjoy the shortest version of the run because it involved deploying game-breaking exploits, namely leaps through walls and long jumps bypassing locked doors without the need to obtain hidden keys.

Settling in, I had one monitor displaying the chat log and the other exhibiting the gameplay so that I might catch every angle of the run without missing important reactions from viewers on stream. The channel had been online for 51 minutes and 26 seconds, and it had reached a viewer count of 466, with more continually arriving. I watched intently for Simply's next move. "That dive, wtf!", a viewer named Puncayshun suddenly exclaimed. "Yea, I only do that dive if I have good enough ghost "rng", Puncay.[11] You'll always have enough speed. It's like the fastest movement you can do there", Simply responded. Somehow, Simply was able to read and respond to his live chat while maintaining his unbroken focus on gameplay. He explained to Puncayshun about the ghosts in the current Mario world, which follow randomly generated patrol patterns that fortuitously can be exploited given some luck and apparently a lot of practice.

Puncayshun, unlike most other viewers, was named a moderator on Simply's channel, as indicated by his exclusive green sword badge next to his screen name in chat. His elevated status, however, did not necessarily distinguish him significantly since there were many other moderators also present on stream (indeed, another moderator made a comment only seconds later). What distinguished Puncayshun, and certainly what commanded Simply's attention, was that he was the current world record holder for 120-star. To be sure, it was commonplace in the wider *Super Mario 64* community for the top competitive players to watch each other on streams, to learn from each other's movement, and to converse on emerging strategies as well as to offer tips; nonetheless, having the current world champion scrutinizing one's play was always a momentous occasion. Each player, after all, harboured a secret jealousy towards Puncayshun (some not so secret), wanting themselves to someday be crowned the best.

Puncayshun was impressed by Simply's movement. Perhaps he was intrigued to learn more about the ghost tactic. More likely, I suspected, he feared that his position as record holder may not last the hour. It was at this point that I made my usual introductions to the stream and offered my own well wishes to Simply in chat: "Hey Simply, glad to see you again, gl on the run".[12] "Hey, what's up. Thank you for the good luck man", he replied to my delight. While I was thrilled to be acknowledged on stream, my moment in the spotlight did not last long. Simply returned almost immediately to addressing Puncayshun. He was eager to discuss an important matter of some growing concern: "Puncay, do you have any controllers that you'd be willing to give me that are as good as the one you gave me? This one ... it still works and stuff ... but it is starting to get to the point where every time I move it has just got a ton of grind. It's just a lot of grinding. I could try cleaning it out, but if that doesn't work then I should get a new controller soon".

Recall that *Super Mario 64* was first published in 1996, decades prior. It was also the launch title for the Nintendo 64 Entertainment System, making the controller, its plastic structure, its buttons, and its mechanical joysticks very old. In fact, it was plausible that Simply's controller was even older than a good portion of his current viewer base; certainly, it had served at the helm of Nintendo 64 video games since before a few of them had grown old enough to call themselves gamers. Due to this, the maintenance of vital components is now of the utmost consequence. It was also a matter of significant financial consideration, as one inquiring viewer later revealed that the current market rate for a new and fully packaged controller could fetch over 200 USD.

For my part, I commented briefly in chat that it might be easier to clean one of the many controllers Simply already owned or perhaps that there

104 Ludic divides

FIGURE 4.3 Simply's many Nintendo controllers.

might be a cheaper source yet to be discovered where he could procure a new one (Figure 4.3). "Ya, I'll try cleaning it and I'll get back to you on that. I could buy my own controller but … It's kind of … There's definitely … I'll go to my retro games store. If they don't have any, then I'll buy one from Puncay. If he doesn't have any, then I'll buy it from Ebay. From Puncay or the store, I know it's good, but on Ebay I can't know if it's any good. That's the problem", Simply explained his complicated dilemma.

At this point, I switched rather reluctantly to a second tab on my browser and began simultaneously watching Simply's stream along with Liveegg's. Liveegg had been streaming for 6 hours and 23 minutes that day, several hours longer than Simply. I considered that it might be instructive to compare the two speedrunners at the same time, an opportunity that was rarely afforded to me on most other field visits. The *Super Mario 64* speedrunning category on Twitch consisted of a very small and closely linked assembly of gamers. Most streamers were not only aware of the others delivering similar content, but they considered each other as colleagues, even close friends. It was for this reason that Liveegg normally tended to broadcast his runs very late at night and into the early morning so as not to compete for viewers against the likes of Simply or any of the other speedrunners.

Henry_92 remarked first in Liveegg's stream, "I was 2 years old when this game got out, though to me the graphics don't get better than this". To which, Go_Mango replied; "Welcome to a 19-year-old game. I was 5

Ludic divides **105**

and it kicked my ass for at least 2 years. Now these guys are doing it in less than 2 hours". While I was amused and could relate to these moments of shared nostalgia (albeit I was quite a bit older when *Mario 64* was released), I noticed that the mood on Liveegg's stream was again distressed:

Aug 11 11:27:20 <zionchar11>	Shit
Aug 11 11:27:24 <zionchar11>	more reset
Aug 11 11:27:25 <zionchar11>	WHY EGG
Aug 11 11:27:37 <joshuarrr_felton>	because cameraman caught him
Aug 11 11:28:34 <joshuarrr_felton>	Its okay we gont this
Aug 11 11:28:38 <joshuarrr_felton>	got*
Aug 11 11:28:51 <void646>	Lol
Aug 11 11:28:56 <zionchar11>	BibleThump NOW PLEASE BEAT THE GAME
Aug 11 11:29:07 <go_mango>	Egg, this is your mother, if you don't get the urn of lifetime going, you're going to bed without supper.
Aug 11 11:30:13 <ythaaker>	Alright now its getting boring sorry
Aug 11 11:31:42 <go_mango>	I dunno what's more determination, the fact you can do that for 6 hours, or that we can watch

The viewers were upset that Liveegg had reset his game. They were especially disheartened that this was happening so late in his stream. "Because the camera man caught him", user joshuarrr_felton defended. "NOW PLEASE BEAT THE GAME", another viewer replied immediately following. Several viewers in chat clearly appeared to be at the limit of their tolerance for the day. The viewer Ythaaker states frankly, "alright now it's getting boring, sorry", whereas Go_Mango quipped: "I dunno what's more determination, the fact you can do that for 6 hours, or that we can watch.

Liveegg's chat continued along similar lines as others debated their reasons for continuing to watch. There was ultimately some consensus from several viewers that they must continue because it was their duty to be present and ready to witness in case of a personal best or world record run. These viewers felt that they could not risk missing that special moment, one that was assuredly going to be an important milestone in what they perceived to be a part of video game history.[13] It was important to persevere. I noted in the margins of my fieldnotes for the day: "living the dream". This was a reminder for myself to compare my observations that were cropping up that day in relation to those I observed elsewhere. The *Super Mario 64*

106 Ludic divides

speedrunners formed an intensely loyal group. The runs they exhibit on stream evoke, or rather reveal, a unique mindset and one of a gamer's positionality that shows aspirations towards greatness—living the dream—as well as reverence for a gamer's role in forging the course of gaming history.

When contrasted with Liveegg, Simply was less forthcoming in making any grand pronouncements or even minor observations about gaming or streaming. He was, as established, one of the most skilled and well-respected gamers in his own right, but he was also often very silent and reluctant to volunteer his insights to me directly. Simply seemed largely disinterested in, or at least discreet about, matters not directly concerned with improving his gameplay tactics. He was, as should be no surprise, completely dedicated to refining his craft and skill, but this regrettably made him more of a challenge and largely unavailable as an informant.

Simply's intensity towards the game (and only matters related to the game) was, however, why Liveegg and many others looked up to him. It was not because he was their senior—they were all roughly the same age in their early to mid-20s—but because Simply's gameplay seemed to represent an ultimate achievement and one that they all seemed to lack but to which they could nevertheless continue striving. Someday, perhaps Liveegg too might replicate with such precision a successful high jump in the lava sea, to long jump the way Simply does across the drawbridge past Lakipu in under 12 seconds, to wall jump the crazy maze without missing the elevator platform, or to slide kick the princess' secret slide. "Simply is great because his movement is "god-tier". If you look and really pay attention to what he is doing, you don't see anything crazy. You see something simple. You see something refined", Liveegg described to me on stream with significant admiration and respect.

I clicked to return to Simply's stream. I noticed his clock had now ticked past 1 hour and 20 minutes, and I scanned quickly across to see the times of his splits thus far. Simply had saved a lot more time while I was watching Liveegg's channel, 39 seconds in total. With only two more worlds remaining until completion, he had already obtained 94 power stars. Most outstandingly, he was for the first time since the start of his stream at a world record pace. Simply suddenly broke his relative silence and concentration: "Awe ... I can't believe how sloppy I am playing!" It seemed like only a microsecond passed when he made a fatal mistake that ended his apparently flawless run.

"Okie dokie". Simply dropped his controller and hit the reset button on the game console, prompting a final end to his attempt. "I can't play with this controller. It got really bad on this run. I don't really know if I can continue playing with this". Both streamers, Liveegg and Simply, were now clearly defeated. While Liveegg would continue speedrunning, Simply, unexpectedly, did not. Instead, and to my surprise, the nearly 500 viewers in chat remained as Simply switched off his Nintendo and proceeded to take apart his controller live on camera. He began the cleaning process. "Dude, you'll void your warranty", one viewer cautioned. Another apparently annoyed but nevertheless continuing to watch remarked next; "What the fuck is this, nice SPEEDGAME man". Yet another viewer commented in jest "WR for cleaning controller starts now!?" I wondered at this point. Was cleaning a controller in view of hundreds of gamers truly "living the dream"?

"Living the dream" was a phrase I discovered very early on in my field-work on one of Liveegg's streams. The topic of that day was centered on what it took to become the best gamer at any particular point in history. One of Liveegg's viewers asked, "Egg is streaming your "job"? Do you have school or work? If not, you're living the dream!" Liveegg's response ultimately engaged a long and drawn-out discussion about expectations and dreams, one that continued as a theme even across multiple days of streaming. Liveegg shared with us that he earned no more than 15 USD of advertisement revenue for a six-hour long broadcast and that most of his income came from subscription fees, to which Twitch claimed 50% of the revenue. He added that this was not including any additional direct dona-tions through PayPal, where he lost another 15% cut for the exchange. "Obviously it's not like a job or whatever, but it's 15 bucks and it adds up when all you do is play games all day", Liveegg remarked in his character-istic self-disparaging tone. "It's barely anything. It's definitely not 'living the dream' … The dream for me is a consistent viewer base so my viewer count isn't always jumping around drastically and also that more people who watch me stay for just me instead of for what I stream. I feel like the major-ity of people just watch me because I'm good at Mario", Liveegg continued.

A few viewers made note of how they felt 15 USD was an acceptable pay-out: "15 dollars per stream is tight, that's food bb!" Others concurred, "Ya that sounds about right, pretty good!" Liveegg himself believed that what he was doing was not sustainable, but he nevertheless did not blame others for his hardships and low-dollar returns. Instead, he felt that success was al-ways within his reach; indeed, it could be obtained by anyone with enough determination and hard work. There were a few, however, who added an important qualifier: "30 [years old] in Esports is retiring age ☹", one viewer claimed. Another replied more optimistically: "We are the generation that will determine how old gamers get". To which still others quickly countered again: "But 30 years old might as well be 90! We can't game past that". Liveegg con-curred with the more negative evaluation. He found that the limits of his own dream would soon be approaching: "What are any of us dude … We're all just little tiny insignificant specs in the universe with a short life-span". Two viewers put a stop to this opining and brought some levity back to the stream: "Why are you going all Aristotle on us?" "Ya, Egg, please you are too deep".

Charity Streams

> All we really want in the end is just acceptance from others and acknowledgement that who we are and what we do is actually worth something (Anonymous Gamer)

What happens to "participatory culture" when corporations start to take notice and begin to impose new models of profitability on emerging communities? We saw through Annie how such efforts, when they go ill prepared, can promptly meet with failure as gamers resist exterior monetization and profit-sharing schemes, especially when those schemes are perceived to be misaligned to their best interests. At the same time, gamers streaming on Twitch exhibit in their discourse and through their actions just how precarious work can be on a live streaming platform, how vulnerable their bargaining positions are, and indeed, they display a distinct naiveite towards their outlook on the future and their plans for obtaining financial independence.

CLOSE-UP: "PARTICIPATORY CULTURE"

The concept of "Participatory Culture" is strongly associated with media scholar Henry Jenkins, but it has been taken up widely within the field of media and cultural studies. Jenkins argues that participatory culture can be seen in various fan communities where fans don't just consume media but actively participate by creating fan fiction, making fan films, or producing fan art, for example.[14] Jenkins also insists that this shift from passive to active engagement has profound educational implications, as participatory culture fosters skills that are valuable in the modern world. I argue in this chapter that this concept also bears significance in the realms of work, philanthropy, and the foundations of the live streaming and gaming communities, but the question of who participates and who profits is a source of contention.

In their annual report for 2015, Twitch proudly announced that their peak monthly broadcasters (unique streamers) had reached over two million. Further, they revealed some truly astronomical numbers to match: over nine billion total messages had been sent, and 241 billion minutes had been watched by an average concurrent viewer count of 550,000. Perhaps most noteworthy of all (especially for Amazon shareholders at the time), the average monthly minutes watched per unique viewer reached 421.6 minutes, surpassing even the video giant YouTube, which only saw its user base consume 291 minutes.[15] Amidst this sea of activity, it was not only the consumer corporations and their marketers who went in search of their share of the profits; notably, non-profits and charitable organizations also went prospecting. Gamers on Twitch and their "participatory cultures" grew entangled not only with profit sharing but also with fund-raising drives to address humanitarian causes.

Charity streams in 2015 on Twitch raised 17,400,000 USD for over 55 charities; notably, "Extra Life" raised $7 million for *Children's Miracle Network*, "Games Done Quick" drew over $2.8 million for the *Prevent Cancer Foundation* and *Doctors Without Borders*, and "Gaming for Good" solicited over $1.3 million in donations towards *Save the Children*.[16] For the *Mario 64* runners, however, the biggest charity event of the year was always, without question, "Games Done Quick". This was a semi-annual stream, one held in the winter and the other during the summer, featuring speedrunners of a wide diversity of video games, each competing to have their speedruns raise the most funds for charity. The "Games Done Quick" streams (GDQs) were designed as marathon events. Live streams would typically run continually for a six-day period, airing video games and game commentary for 24 hours each day. The GDQs were extremely successful and popular in 2015 (Figure 4.4), usually culminating in a feature speedrun of Mario near the end of the broadcast, which nearly everyone looked forward to watching.

It was the likes of Simply, Liveegg and others who would be the stars of the GDQ show. They would routinely draw crowds of viewers in attendance, often surpassing 150,000 on the channel. More importantly, these streamers also brought in the largest donations, sometimes reaching into the tens of thousands of dollars raised before even the capture of the first power star in the game.

It was July 29th, 2015. Summer Games Done Quick was only just beginning to build up speed on Day 3 of the marathon event. At 9:27 a.m. GMT, I tuned in to the stream, preparing myself for another full day of participant observation. These events only return twice per year, so I was eager to witness as much as possible live on stream. During these events, I had grown accustomed to going offline only when I needed to sleep or to prepare meals. Being still early in the morning and midway through the week's marathon, I noticed the viewer count of only 82,386 viewers in the chat was comparatively low compared to other scheduled times. A streamer called Sylux98 was speedrunning the game Sonic the Hedgehog: Triple Trouble. Much to the disappointment of long-time fans, rival Sega Games Company in the late 1980s and

110 Ludic divides

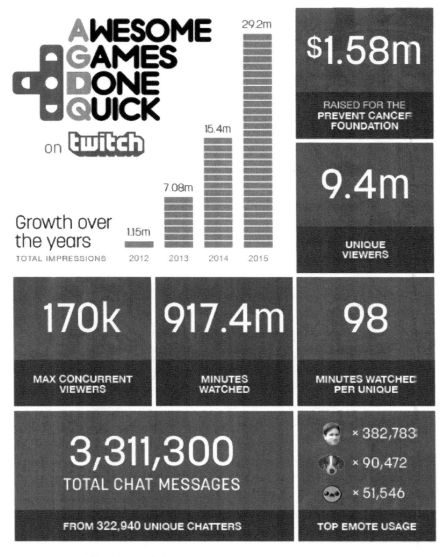

FIGURE 4.4 AGDQ Twitch Stats.

early 1990s never accumulated anywhere near the fandom of the Super Mario Brothers. Although also historic, Sonic the Hedgehog simply could not draw the same crowds, and I suspected that the same gap in popularity existed at the time of the event given the relatively low number of gamers tuning in. Nevertheless, Sylux98 was estimated to complete his run in under 25 minutes, and his fans in chat were already commenting boisterously.

At that time, the donation total for this run's marathon had reached 358,033 USD, and Sylux98 was visibly nervous. We could hear some hesitation in his voice as he diligently explained to viewers his strategies and tactics of play. During marathon events, dozens of donations are processed throughout the course of any given speedrun, and so donation messages that may be attached are pulled at random and read aloud, usually during moments of pause in the speedrunner's game commentary. "There's not too much to say here. If you have any donations, you can go ahead and take care of them", Sylux signalled to the GDQ host, indicating that she may begin reading one of said donation messages: "Alright, thank you! So, we have a 20-dollar donation from Raft250 who says; I am super excited for the classic sonic block and what better way to lead it off than the great Sylux. Keep it up my speedrunners!" The host of the stream continued, taking it upon herself to read an even longer list of subsequent donations:

We have a 50-dollar donation from a viewer who says; I am a first-time watcher of GDQ but avid follower. I am loving the content and thanks everyone for playing towards such a great cause. This next one says; I grew up on the 'blue blur', so I found it appropriate to donate during the Sonic block. Keep up the good work! We've got to go fast! And we have another 30-dollar donation from a viewer who says; I had to donate during *Triple Trouble*. I completely forgot about this game but played it so much as a kid.

Sylux98 was soon approaching his final blow to the end-game boss called the Atomic Destroyer. He piloted Sonic in a characteristic "spin dash" also known informally as the "blue blur" to make his eventual overwhelming blow. "And …… time!" Sylux signalled the end of his run.

Sylux98 was met with enthusiastic applause (mostly in virtual onstream), as the video panned to a wide-angle camera view of the venue's physical location. Most of the seats in the function room of the hotel they had rented were yet to be filled. Presumedly, many were still sleeping in their rooms upstairs after a very late night of speedrunning. There were 91,672 viewers in chat. Smaller numbers notwithstanding, they brought more than enough energy to cheer on the upcoming runners. The host again proceeded to read several more donation messages:

Let's catch up on a few donations while we are between runs. We have a 50-dollar donation that says; first time donator and longtime watcher,

112 Ludic divides

so many wonderful games and runners for such a real cause. I missed some of the early runs due to work, but you can be sure I'll be waking up at 3am for the super stars saga run! Hype!" Next, we have a 30-dollar donation from a viewer who says you guys are an inspiration to speedrunners everywhere. Keep up the hard work! And we have a 50-dollar donation from a viewer who says; I've always been a big fan of GDQ, maybe I'll try a speedrun one day, glad to support a great cause!

Wishing to acknowledge the importance of the event for new and upcoming speedrunners, the GDQ host paused her reading of donations. We learn from GDQ runners, the host explained. We see how to execute difficult "strats" (strategies) while also planning how to strive towards improvements in our own creative use of game play.

It was during the breaks between scheduled speedruns that event organizers set out on runs of their own, setting up new game consoles, testing the equipment, and ushering in players to their positions on the set couches. In later years, after my departure from the field, the GDQ event organizers added specialist game analysts and professional commentators to fill these gaps in airtime. During the 2015 marathon runs, however, viewers on the stream were entreated almost entirely to donor messages as these were read to the tune of retro gaming music. In all, the earlier GDQ productions were very nostalgic for older gamers, those who could remember playing *Sonic* or *Mario* in their distant childhood. We see a lot of excitement in the messages from donors who are overjoyed to be able to catch the live show and happy to be capable of donating towards what is, assuredly, a good cause.

The GDQ host helped to clarify where those donation dollars were headed and what the mission statement of the charity *Medicins Sans Frontier* (Doctors Without Borders, DWB) set out to do. She explained that DWB was an international medical humanitarian organization providing aid in nearly 70 countries. Rather hurriedly, she read from her statement how those dollars would help people whose survival is threatened by violence, neglect, or catastrophe primarily due to armed conflict, exclusions from healthcare, natural disasters, or malnutrition. DWB, she continued to read, provides independent, impartial assistance, brings attention to neglected crises, challenges inadequacies, and highlights abuses.

I reflected at this point on how we were to assume that there could be no inconsistencies in those mandates, but I soon discovered that not many others (if there were any at all) were actually listening very closely. One viewer remarked, "What is she saying?", perhaps genuinely curious to know more or merely a benign troll replying flippantly as the rest of the chat appeared disinterested and disengaged. I saw only one quick reply: "It's the charity thing. She's talking about the charity. Whatever. Anyway, what's the next speedrun?"

Conclusion: Ludic Divides

The GDQ charity streams remain an unqualified "good" for humanitarian causes, but in 2015 they were not altogether unproblematic for the gamers who established and maintained the streaming communities that made it all possible. It was clear to me after concluding observations that viewers certainly felt inspired by all the speedrunning taking place, but there was a distinct tension between feeling good about the main event—a celebration about achieving gaming feats—versus feeling good about the charity as an impetus to raising money for Doctors Without Borders. Games Done Quick broke several records in 2015, the most lauded of which was its fundraising record across all the events, reaching 2.8 million USD. The stream had grown exponentially year over year leading up to GDQ 2015, which marked the best retrospective increase by far, having nearly doubled its total impressions for viewers watching and commenting in chat. These were, however, not intrinsically speedrunning records. These were, in effect, Twitch marketing records more akin to corporate numbers reporting to Amazon and shareholders how the growing platform was generating some positive worth.

After the marathon's conclusion, I interviewed my core Super Mario 64 participants, including Liveegg and Simply. I gathered their impressions on the GDQ proceedings. Liveegg could not attend in person, but he had broadcast a message of support from his own Twitch channel. Simply participated in a three-way race along with another speedrunner at the physical event. Much to my own exhilaration as a witness, Simply, who was one of my closest participants, had won the grand finale of the Mario 64 race in front of a viewer audience of over 165 thousand. Each speedrunner reported to me how enthusiastic and thrilled they were to be together on such a high-profile stage, but there was some detectable weariness in their recounting of the monumental events. Games Done Quick was only one of several other charity streams in which they had participated. They recounted how nice it was to take a break from the usual daily grind of streaming to visit charity marathons where they could finally meet up with friends to "relax" and "just hang out". Not all charity streams raise nearly as much money as does GDQ, but these were joyous moments for the wider community and a time to gather and assemble in celebration of the speedrunning games. GDQ, though, was perceived as being more "corporate" than the others. As one participant speedrunner explained, "the

114 Ludic divides

charity is just like a side thing we do". GDQ should "focus more on the community, not the donations".

Some felt that what gamers were doing at GDQ was a version of "selling out", that they were giving up for charity, their sense of community, their hard work, perhaps even their living dreams. These were indeed worthy causes; nonetheless, they were of a recognizable corporate structure to which gamers did not feel especially attached or proud. In effect, if streamers and their viewers were primarily interested in a game, they did so as a community. Feeling good about the game was feeling good about relationships with others and to the game. However, the monetization of Twitch and its charity events introduces a complexity to the making of a community that encroaches upon a gamer's freedom and ability to define values and keep control of their own narratives, keeping the focus on the needs and interests of gaming.

In closing, I understand the digital dilemma of this chapter as one being born of "ludic divides", which like "the Zap" is to emphasize the points of fracture when a gamer's uncompromising dedication to a strictly playful quality of life—a life devoted primarily to gaming—gives way to concessions made to outside interests. Such compromises are often in service to those who are less reverent of video games or those who do not share in a celebration of gaming. We saw with Annie how measures of corporate infiltration can meet with failure on Twitch when developers "dive in" for profit with little to no regard for the needs of actual gamers. A corporation in its own right, the GDQs have recently met with a similar end when compared to Annie's company.

The GDQ charity marathon events have extracted the most that they can from gamers and streamers, but there has been a clear cost to this process of monetization. The most recent data on concurrent viewership has indicated a significant decline. From its peak during the Covid-19 pandemic in 2020, with a maximum concurrent viewer count of over 230,000, GDQ fell in 2021, dropping to only 141,000 concurrent viewers, and again in 2022, plummeting to only 113,000.[17] There are a variety of explanations for this attrition, not the least of which was the attempts from organizers to run the events during a global pandemic when the necessary "in person" components were lacking, yet I submit that the true cause is more systemic in nature. The days of exponential growth for all charity initiatives on Twitch have ended. The recent GDQ decline has happened not because of global catastrophe but as a consequence of gamers having been asked to labor for too long while simultaneously being kept "too thin". Gamers, as a consequence of their ludic divides, or "the zap" as we historically understand it, have had their communities thoroughly tapped.

Streamers and viewers find themselves drained from their participation. They are losing their joy and dedication to streaming as outside interests—charitable interests—forcefully push in.

QUESTIONS

1. What is a "ludic divide"?
2. In what ways do viewers on live streams assist with the production of a stream? How valuable is their labor on Twitch?
3. Why might corporations be so interested in partnering with gamers and streamers? What do corporations stand to gain? What do gamers stand to gain? What does each stand to lose?

Notes

1 Cohen, S. (1984). ZAP! The Rise and Fall of Atari. New York: McGraw-Hill.
2 Sheff, D. (1993). Game Over: How Nintendo Zapped an American Industry, Captured Your Dollars, and Enslaved Your Children. New York: Random House.
3 See: Kücklich, J. (2005). "Precarious Playbour: Modders and the Digital Games Industry"; and Dyer-Witheford N., & Peuter G. (2009). Games of Empire: Global Capitalism and Video Games. Minneapolis: University of Minnesota Press.
4 My notion of "ludic divide" emphases a point of fracture when a gamer's uncompromising dedication to gaming and to a playful quality of life comes under tension from the pressures of outside interests. I should note that this notion is different from longstanding contestations in game studies between two founding schools of thought, the "ludologists" and the "narratologist". The "ludologists" take up the position that game studies ought to be a study of game-based elements, design, and simulation. Ludologists insist that game studies consider game elements of ludology *a priori* drawing a strict boundary of what can legitimately be contained within the discipline of game studies. See: Aarseth, E. (2004). "Genre Trouble" in Electronic Book Review, May 21, 2004. The "narratologists", on the other hand, consider the aesthetic and hermeneutic qualities of gaming as these pertain to narrative. I find that there is merit to each perspective since both can texture our consideration of ethnographic accounts. For a more balanced perspective on genre troubles in game studies, see: Voorhees, G. (2019) "Genre Troubles in Game Studies: Ludology, Agonism, and Social Action" in Journal of Media Studies and Popular Culture, Special Issue, May 2019.
5 Twitch has a policy and code of conduct that explicitly prohibits unsolicited offers on live-streams.
6 The world record at the time for completing the game and piloting Mario towards acquiring all 120 stars was an astonishing 1 hour, 39 minutes and 21 seconds.

7 A close analogue to this time keeping can be found in any telecast of a marathon run or indeed other sporting events featuring games with several splits during the course of normal play, such as for example in tennis or curling.

8 Most famously, "do what you love" is an interpretation of Confucius' words "Choose a job you love, and you will never have to work a day in your life".

9 The EgguOgre tended on Liveegg's channel to be reserved only for the most frustrating moments. All partnered Twitch channels gain access to a series of fully customizable emoticons or emojis for their subscribed viewers to react in chat. Each partner tends to design these to suit the character and content of a community stream. In the case for Liveegg, they did not entirely reflect only the Mario universe but as well included his character interests from other areas of popular culture including animated films. There were six exclusive emojis for Liveegg at the time of fieldwork.

10 Permanent channel names were largely enforced on Twitch as an administrative measure to facilitate smoother revenue share payments as well as to more easily trace a channel's history over longer periods of time. Permanent names also ensured that streamers who grew to foster much larger communities could not change identities.

11 * wtf—"what the fuck"; rng—"random number generation".

12 gl—good luck.

13 Liveegg often lectured at great length about the historical timeline of Super Mario 64 speedruns. He referred to important stretches in history as "eras" and was very clear on the minute details which separated the runners who belonged to each segment. For example, most of the current speedrunners at the time of my fieldwork felt they owed great homage to the "Siglemic Era", a time when the American player Siglemic first massively popularized the practice of speedrunning the game on Twitch, importing many of his movements from the already established Japanese speedrunning community in the late 2000s and adding his own strategies.

14 Jenkins, H (2006). Fans Bloggers and Gamers. New York (NY): New York University Press.

15 Twitch (2016) Accessed 4/23/2016 URL: http://www.twitch.tv/p/about

16 Ibid. Twitch (2016)

17 An, Y. (2023). "AGDQ 2023: Viewership Analytics" on GameSight Accessed 12/4/2023 URL: https://blog.gamesight.io/awesome-games-done-quick-viewership-analytics-2023/

CONCLUSION

Live Video Politics

Introduction

Reality has a limits. During the closing weeks of finishing field work for this book, the most unlikely of my computer peripherals began showing signs of failure. My mouse, faithful though it had been serving for millions of clicks for over a decade, was suddenly beginning to miss-track on its pad.[1] The buttons, now visibly worn, began to stick, and the braided cable that was originally designed to help withstand the test of time began showing significant fraying, slowly unravelling at its base. The solution to the problem was simple—I needed to purchase a new, top-of-the-line device. After all, this technology (along with my keyboard) is fundamental to my being able to grow close to gaming communities online. My mouse is my primary conduit for connecting and grounding me, much as a controller or a joystick is for others.

The replacement I decided to purchase, hefty and pricey at 79.99 USD, would, with any luck, serve me better and usher me into yet another decade of gaming and research. I acquired the *Steelseries Rival 600*, and its arrival on my desk would prove to be timely. As I opened the packaging, the text on the box included surprising marketing scripts:

RISE UP!

We don't play games to escape reality. We play to rewrite it.
We're the Esports professionals and the pubstars.

118 Conclusion

The 1hp heroes and the bottom of the scoreboard zeros.
The streamers and the dreamers.
Whether you win, lose or ragequit—that's all on you.
But remember that **reality is not a limit.**
GLHF[2]

(*Rival* 600, Steelseries, 2018)

The *Rival 600* packaging commands gamers to "RISE UP! We don't play games to escape reality. We play to rewrite it". It was at this point that I rolled my eyes at the sight of yet another gamification and commodification, a hapless example of corporate sloganeering that *Steelseries* calculated gamers would respond favourably to. I looked closer. At the bottom of the box, there appeared to be a portrait of Sumail, the Esports professional gamer, and a key subject to recall from Chapter 2 of this book. He is standing next to his coach, Charlie Yang, as both are turning away from the cameras to greet a massive crowd of cheering fans. Sumail's image is captured from his *Dota 2* game world video. He has supposedly transcended its limits, helping his team achieve victory and take home a portion of the nearly 18 million USD prize pool. I notice the smallest of details: Sumail is shown wearing number 01 on his team sports shirt, emulating the team numbers worn by other mainstream competitive athletes; the American flag stitched to his jersey above his name immediately recalls the carefully crafted narrative of his emigration from Pakistan, the country of his birth, to Rosemount, Minnesota, the land of his gaming opportunity; and finally, the many corporate sponsors and logos, prominent among them *Steelseries* but also, notably, *Xfinity*, a trade name of Comcast Cable Communications, as well as *Scuf Gaming*, a company that handcrafts and customizes other professional controllers and video game peripherals. Was this image meant to depict reality? More importantly, was this mouse meant to help myself or other gamers transcend our limits and also become wealthy and successful Esports champions like Sumail?

As it turns out, my computer mouse revealed itself to be a surprise conduit of a very different kind. It was a reminder that reality is a limit not only for gamers but for everyone, chiefly because we cannot ever fully escape into our communities online. Online sociality, whether it be live streaming on Twitch or gaming within the boundaries of a virtual world, is always grounded by the material conditions that make such relations possible. The material conditions of life, as my old mouse in its worn-out state attests, are not just a limit; they were for me the singular limit, a physicality and an inseparable part of gaming that was ultimately impossible to ignore. From this final vignette, I begin to introduce the main conclusion of this book, namely that there are limits in reality and that the Gamer Citizen forms

Conclusion **119**

relationships within those bounds to enact what I call "live-video politics" on Twitch. By politics, I mean relations of power in the affairs of people living everyday life in a community. By live-video politics, I mean relations of power between gamers living and streaming in a digital age on Twitch.

Inhabiting Home

A first dimension of live video politics on Twitch entails the building, maintaining, as well as occasional defending of "home". In this conclusion, I come to understand "home" to signify a community or channel where regular viewers attend to routine business and help facilitate the base affective qualities of a broadcast. An important premise for this is that streaming is not a game. It is instead a system that, among other outcomes, involves the most mundane of daily interactions, such as greeting viewers and inquiring about activities throughout the day, yet also occasionally involves attending special events, reinforcing ties, and sustaining a connection that extends offline. Streaming on Twitch is primarily rooted in the virtual worlds of video games, but these communities are not to be conceptualized as being limited or devoid of human contact. To the contrary, these are communities that are characterized by their vibrancy and close attention to the complete lives of the many members, followers, subscribers, and general viewers who contribute in valuable and diverse ways. From the start, as a researcher studying the politics and communities of streaming, I was welcomed by my participants onto their channels and into this shared space that they called home. This was often about learning the features and techniques of their favourite video games, including all the usual core developments such as character selection, beautifully rendered environments, and other gameplay mechanics, but it was also about being made to feel a part of a wider network of people, each of us being a gamer who seeks to go beyond the basic functionality of gameplay and establish in its place something more expansive and more durable. Inhabiting home, as such, is about generating a sense of self online that is fundamentally inclusive of others and involves, in different ways, an established cohabitation or dwelling.

Sometimes, inhabiting home on Twitch means conquering enemies together in a competitive match; other times, it means exploring entirely new game modes, delving deeply into a dungeon or performing an exciting speedrun. Still other times, one might find home under attack. Inhabiting a home is also about sustaining that home and defending against hostile and invasive others, agitators in the live chat who aim to sow discord and spread malice for their own purposes. During less dramatic moments, inhabiting home might occasionally mean taking the time to repair a broken-down controller, ensuring that each component is well greased and

120 Conclusion

reassembled to its proper specifications. Home might be a place to opine about life philosophy and to spread advice to fellow gamers on which future paths to take amidst a plethora of divergent choices. Indeed, at any given moment, our feelings at home could range from total banality to the utmost volatility and even reach the profound. We might debate together about what was the latest obsession for top streamers on Twitch—the likes of, for example, the streamer called xQc, who made history by streaming himself challenging a chess grandmaster called Hikaru. There could be stirrings at home surrounding the latest celebrity gossip. What was the news about the Red Bull-fuelled streamer Ninja? Would he sign a new contract on a rival platform for the rumoured 100 million USD payout that was reported in the news? I knew more than a few gamers who proclaimed not to care much about such larger-than-life personalities, and yet it was those same gamers who attended convention events such as TwitchCon and WonderCon, where they lined up for hours awaiting the chance to purchase an autograph or take a picture with a streaming star. Finding home on Twitch means sharing a small corner of this website alongside giants of gaming, streaming professionals, and Esports champions who draw viewership numbering in the tens of thousands. More often, however, home simply means taking up a smaller residence on Twitch, finding a quiet corner where one can relax, get to know regular followers, learn more about video games in common, or exchange stories about work and/or study as well as other facets of daily life. In sum, home is where the streaming is. Importantly, live video politics is foremost about gamers finding ways to inhabit home together.

Writing Back

A second dimension of live video politics involves the reclaiming of identity and the reinventing of the gamer subject. On June 18th, 2018, the World Health Organization published revisions for the international Statistical Classification of Diseases called the ICD-11 that included a featured emphasis on "internet gaming disorder". The ICD-11 is the latest iteration in an extensive list of classifications that has been in development for several decades. On the web document's portal, the following statement serves as an introduction to health practitioners, policymakers, and laypeople alike:

> Ready for the 21st century …, WHO [The World Health Organization] released a version of ICD-11 to allow Member States time to plan implementation … this version is a vast improvement on ICD-10. First, it has been updated for the 21st century and reflects critical advances in science and medicine. Second, it can now be well integrated with electronic health applications and information systems. This new version is fully

electronic, significantly easier to implement which will lead to fewer mistakes, allows more detail to be recorded, all of which will make the tool much more accessible, particularly for low-resource settings ...[3]

A cursory glance at the website does appear to indicate a finely tuned database and one apparently ready for the 21st century. With no credentials required and no fees necessary, it is possible to easily follow a chain of hyperlinks to find a particular disease of interest and read its classification, including associated conditions, related symptoms, and a preliminary suggested plan for treatment. Gaming disorder is listed on 6C51 under the parent category of "disorders due to addictive behaviors". Within its description, the organization is careful to stipulate that only such cases that have been tracked for a period exceeding twelve months may qualify as gaming addiction, and even then only if the activity under question remains extensive enough to infringe upon the "normal" functioning of daily tasks and associations. The gamer is considered to have a disorder if his or her performance of sustained gameplay leads to shifting other vital responsibilities to the periphery. What is more, there must be "impaired control of these behaviours" such that the gamer elects to continue gaming despite known and expected detrimental effects to their personal wellbeing. The World Health Organization insists that the inclusion of any disorder—especially those less well understood and/or understudied—is disseminated to stimulate ongoing debate in the academic and healthcare communities. The ICD is designed to be a tool for servicing those less well-resourced settings, namely psychiatry and other therapy institutions. For the ICD, all this is to make the claim that gaming is an activity on which it is necessary to impose some considerable sanctions to improve the mental and physical health of gamers who are understood as "at risk".

It is helpful to look closer at the term "sanction". With reference to the newly classified internet gaming disorder, we can clarify at least two meanings of the word. The first is the sense in which "to sanction" implies giving official permission or approval for a scrutinized activity. Such force of authorization usually comes from video game review authorities, regional ratings boards, video game scholars, or expert practitioners, and through their interventions, we see video games classified for use in certain target markets—for example, within the North American region, video games are labelled "E" for everyone, "T" for teens, and "A" for adults. The second meaning in which we use the term "sanction" signifies an imposed penalty of some kind. Here, active sanctioning is found more along the lines of longstanding debates against harmful video games; thus, media reporters, parents, and policy-makers may impose strong warnings against gaming to address what they perceive to be particularly abhorrent and/or dangerous video games. This second form of "sanction" is intended

122 Conclusion

to further restrict the spread of addiction and violence, usually amongst a class of presumed-to-be-young and impressionable gamers. Sanctioning play in either respect, whether it be to control the normal distribution of video games or to outright label an individual game as off-limits, entails consequences not just for theorization but for everyday perception. The effect of sanctioning play in any regard is to further minimize gamer agency, to deny gamers their full autonomy, and to limit the free functioning and flourishing of the gaming community. While I do not argue against the need to review and control certain video game titles as a standard operating practice—especially where children are involved—I do indicate that such sanctioning practices can have lasting effects when we later decide on the limits of acceptability and accountability as they pertain to the health of everyday gamers at any age. To classify gaming as a disorder, even with limited reservations, as the ICD-11 proposes, is reckless because it serves to renew a dominant discourse of disaffection (see Chapter 1). Where violence once held the focus and incited the condemnation of many non-gamers, now mental disorders threatens to supersede all other concerns from outsiders looking at gaming and its growth into live streaming. Thus, the figure of the gamer on Twitch undergoes a process of **"reification"**—they are always and primarily associated with an unhealthy subject.

CLOSE-UP 1: "REIFICATION"

Reification is a process whereby an abstract conception is treated as if it were an existing, real and material thing. Some academic traditions might view this as a fallacy of misplaced concreteness, since concepts ought to remain as tools and not as primary objects of study. In this book, however, reification is intended as an important and central process whereby languages solidify abstract concepts into important aspects of everyday life. Reification establishes our understanding of the reality that we all share. The way discourses come to reify (verb form) certain concepts has tangible implications in the world, both online and offline. These are often seen and experienced through stereotypes, prejudices, discrimination, and other social dynamics.

Overall, sanctioning in this way is detrimental to a wider gamer community since gamer identity is never deemed fully permissible without extensive review and preconditioned doubt. Worse still, the gamer remains constrained by a cognitive standard of "normalcy" in the ICD-11 that appears ill-equipped to handle many of the actual troubles that gamers face in the 21st century.

Despite the ICD-11's stated goal to help practitioners, the troubles streamers and gamers experience on Twitch are both multifarious and complex. These arise not from a failing cognition or from individual mental illness, but from their sociality and in the details of their gaming and streaming activities. Gamers daily encounter negativity and disparagement from others who consider—perhaps for the first time—the prospect of streaming either as a hobby or a full-time profession. For example, Adrian Chen, writing for the *New Yorker*, shares a story of the sometimes lucrative yet often stressful life of a live streamer. His readership ostensibly has little to no familiarity with the subject, yet Chen describes a life for gamers reportedly embedded in cyberspace and now deeply implicated on the level of social and material relations. Unfortunately, it takes only the first four words—"a strange creature stalks"—to reveal the root of Chen's framing. To introduce the streamer, we learn first that he is, as a matter of course, male, pale, tall, and skinny. He is a mess of gadgets and wires, tethering him to a plethora of technical equipment. He is the cyborg that no one ever envisions and the digital influencer that no one wishes for. Increasingly synonymous with the gamer, the streamer, according to Chen, is as reclusive as ever, a "free spirit" who refuses to take on responsibility or conform to the designated parameters of acceptable society. He is not human; instead, he is a "strange creature" who "stalks".[4]

Yet for all the criticism we may level at Chen, what is troubling in his account can also be freeing. In the context of live video politics, gamers on Twitch find an existence in which "there are no more secrets" (Chen), where public personas override private life almost completely. This is not necessarily a weakness, nor is it inherently a failing; gamers find new tools and resources with which to "write back" against the mainstream outlets who demonize and vilify. In live video politics, they find the opportunity to reclaim their identity and to reinvent what it means to be a gamer subject in the 21st century. This movement, as is now accessible and evident for all to see on Twitch, is not entirely a linear process. Rather, it depends on many externalities and layered power mechanisms at play. In live video politics, gamers are only just beginning their struggle for command over discourse, hence the significance and importance of this particular facet of live-video politics, to "write back" against a dominant discourse of disaffection.

124 Conclusion

Spectres at Play

Although on the surface this might appear as a decisive moment when gamers are empowered to reimagine themselves online, leveraging new tools and levels of command, there are two interrupting "spectres at play" they have yet to overcome. The first, as already discussed, is the spectre of a lonely and disaffected gamer subject detached from the social and political world. The second is a spectre not of entrepreneurship, as Julian Kücklich describes in "precarious playbor", but rather a spectre of neoliberalism more akin to what Jim McGuigan elucidates in the "**neo-liberal self**".[5] As they grow more popular, gamers streaming on platforms like Twitch benefit from new opportunities, but they also meet with dilemmas as they find their newfound success systematically vulnerable to capital extraction and private gain. Streaming video games offers a vital point of social contact for some and an intensely affective encounter for others who are actively engaged with the process of making and sustaining communities. Further, we see a sense of duty and dedication to the craft as gamers invest numerous hours of very hard work into their streaming channels, all this to satisfy the ever-present need to become better players and simultaneously to satisfy the expectations of a growing subscriber base. While this sense of duty has fundamentally been about a gamer's dedication to, and expression of, what has become a rich cultural form, it is now entangled with schemes for corporate ownership and control, reenforcing capital ties under the guise of mutually profitable collaboration.

Streamers generate what is increasingly recognized as lucrative content that can be sold or monetized for various external interests. Often, they are called upon to lead an active and critical humanitarianism as they increasingly drive charity initiatives raising tens of millions of dollars each year on Twitch.[6] Gamers are presented with affiliate partnerships with Amazon to assist the parent company in the sale of consumer goods and the spread of an encroaching monopoly over the distribution of those goods worldwide. Additionally, the largest streamers are commonly offered sponsorship contracts, sometimes surpassing 500,000 USD per year, to promote products such as energy drinks and to sell gaming peripherals such as controllers and desk chairs.[7] The spectre of neoliberalism is therefore an insidious haunt always lying in wait. Once thinking of themselves as carefree and uniquely in command of a purely ludic quality of life—a life premised upon playful collectives—gamers are now under pressure to substitute everything for a life that champions self-reliance, free-market capitalism, and private enterprise.

When taken together, the spectres represent a complex amalgam very much akin to what is described elsewhere in video game historiography as the "zap", a phenomenon when gamer communities found their once-untapped entertainment under pressure to be converted into larger-scale profitability in the service of some of the first major video game studios, namely ATARI and later Nintendo Entertainment.[8] Except today, the zap is refined into "cool-capitalism", as McGuigan describes it. Its spectre haunts because the riches and successes gaming and streaming promise to bring are now considered to be "in vogue". Gamers are delighted to view themselves as financially independent and recast in terms of flexibility, adaptability, and personal ownership over successes and failures.[9] It is important to note that very few are impervious to the need to monetize and sustain their community to ultimately ensure a healthy livelihood. Many gamers-turned-streamers on Twitch wholeheartedly consider themselves as working professionals, and the viewers who dutifully follow in support do so with full awareness of themselves as unproblematically paying consumers. This economic and relational shift leaves gamers confronting "ludic divides" as they "go corporate", recalling a worker's history and the age-old struggle for control over conditions of labour.

CLOSE-UP 2: THE "NEO-LIBERAL SELF"

The neo-liberal self describes a kind of individual identity that has imbued characteristics of "neoliberalism", its values, norms, and moral imperatives. Neoliberalism is an economic and political ideology that finds market-driven solutions to be the best course of action. It is a system of ideas that finds societal challenges are best solved through individual responsibility, de-regulation, and privatization. Jim McGuigan is not the first to critique the neo-liberal self, but his work is exemplary in showing how neoliberalism now permeates society so completely that we see it driving cultural spheres as well as economic systems. While the neo-liberal self is perhaps dominant today, it is not inevitable. Calling attention to the struggle over identity and the neo-liberal self generates critical awareness of various important social issues, such as poor mental health, alienation, social injustices, and finally economic exploitation.

To provide content for this analysis, I revisit a gamer and streamer called Liveegg, one of several core participant streamers discussed in

126 Conclusion

this book. Liveegg developed a gamer persona on his live stream as a so-called speedrunner—that is, a gamer who specializes in completing video games in world record time. Liveegg considers himself first and foremost to be a streamer who is dedicated to his viewers, something he has proved on his routine broadcasts time and time again by his readiness to supply advice and provide support to his viewer base. Viewers and followers of the stream were also gamers, many of whom wished to similarly master their play. They would ask Liveegg if they saw a particular new "strat" (strategy) or a new pathway that they did not understand. They sometimes watched to relive their favourite levels of the game or their most memorable final "boss fight". These are clear characteristics of a ludic quality of life in this community, one that is intensely dedicated to a focus on each other and on the core aspects of game play.

Paradoxically, Liveegg often exhibited the competing imperative to appear unconcerned with a wider world beyond his video games. There were several times on stream when he actively ignored the interactions and requests from his viewers in live chat. He appeared at these times hyper-fixed upon refining his own personal gameplay, and this is paradoxical because even in these moments of solitude, Liveegg was also entirely committed to streaming his progress to the benefit of thousands of gamers online. His actions, simply by following through on his commitment to go live and to stream each day, are emblematic of a complete devotion to service and yet also a focus entirely on self.

While they may be tied up within a consumer society and its inevitable links to profit generation, gamers on Twitch reveal that they attempt nevertheless to operate by a different set of rules. Gaming culture still ostensibly stands as a culture that exists independently and remains defiantly non-monetarily driven. The deep engagement and plausible reverence for community history we observe on Twitch reveal a profile of gamers that is in many ways the antithesis of the lone gamer subject. Out of a deep sense of loyalty, they can be intensely supportive of fellow peers who lack acceptance beyond gaming and streaming communities. From this, I can confidently assert that feeling good about a game on Twitch is as much about appreciating relationships with others who feel the same as it is about celebrating more technical gameplay aspects. Live-video politics, then, is about preserving these core emotional, social, and ludic aspects without being overcome by the spectres at play. And yet, free and undirected playfulness in gaming inevitably begins to erode as financial realities set in. Live-video politics, then, is about the ongoing defence of Twitch as a site of struggle where loneliness and free-market capitalism are never conceded completely.

Being Citizens

There have been others who have recently critiqued popular notions of who gamers are and what they are capable of accomplishing. Shira Chess elegantly reframes the discussion by introducing her real-world perspective, capturing the experiences of the many women who play video games. She contrasts these accounts with a theoretical "player two" figure born out of the video game industry's narrow construction of a feminine identity. Chess explores what is often rendered invisible or marginalized. Her work exposes the many disparities that come to light as one pays attention to gender roles and the levels of influence women have over gaming. The hope is that this new perspective may ultimately help to reposition gamer communities and the gaming industry to bring gamers to a place where they are both enabled and emboldened to fashion a healthier and more inclusive "designed identity" for the betterment of future communities.[10]

Indeed, there is much to gain from adopting a feminist perspective. Feminist arguments build upon a rich legacy of standpoint theory and continue to surface in recent work.[11] Amanda Philips, for instance, seeks to revisit the uncomfortable and often turbulent sub-cultures of gaming by diving deeply into the ludic processes of games, exposing the many gendered troubles that gamers face. Indeed, for Philips, the trouble with gender goes beyond merely identifying and condemning unsavoury reputations; she encourages us to challenge our traditional understandings and base assumptions by deploying an intersectional analysis, calling for everyone "to trouble the ways we think about gamers, the ways we write about them, and the ways we ask them to change".[12] While this contributes significantly to a feminist praxis that understands how gender is constructed, represented, and circulated under systems of patriarchy, this is ultimately not to merely dismantle hegemonic forces but to find ways to "game them". It is all too easy to emphasize the many faults and tribulations of male gamers. Philips rightly asks how we might also cultivate each gamer's unique abilities (as any gender, not only women), such as to tap into systems of power, to bend rules, to exploit institutions, and ultimately to find ways of "winning" in a contest of social and political contention.

Finally, Christoper B. Patterson proposes an exploration of a gamer subject who favours bodily sensations. Patterson focuses on a world of gaming that produces an anarchic self, unhinged, messy and at times beyond "political self-depictions".[13] Questioning what happens when we shift our analysis towards stimulating engagements and gaming pleasure,

128 Conclusion

alongside noted critiques of gender, race, and empire, he finds that a gamer's "erotics" liberates the gamer subject to become a subject of disobedience. Gamers may counterintuitively be considered more capable of speaking truth to power, more capable of challenging authority when necessary, and even more capable of reinventing what it fundamentally means to enact radical transformations of the self. Gamers hold the potential to unlock ludic qualities to subsequently unlock something in themselves, perhaps to break free from their stable identities and to see through the ideological structures that come to dominate video game visual and narrative scripts. Gamers, ultimately, become the participants whose very pleasures create the possibilities for political resistance.[14]

Together, these voices form an evolving segment of critical video game studies that serves as a precursor for a final pillar in live-video politics, namely the live-video politics of *being citizens*. As alluded to in Chapter 1 of this book, a significant first step towards that ideal is to acknowledge the depth and complexity of what it means to embody the positionality of being a gamer subject. Keeping the above scholars in mind, I wish to emphasize that those whom I call "gamers" throughout this book are not a monolith—there are many gamers who face multiple and differing oppressions and challenges within distinct gaming communities, not the least of which are premised upon individual subordinations of gender, race, and sexuality—yet I argue that all gamers have more work to do in order to overcome the dominant discourse of disaffection. This work must be done collectively; it is work for all gamers—as citizens—to accomplish.

Firstly, it is time to stop theorizing as if gamers are somehow lost in video games online, looking for a way back to more stable ground. We can accomplish this shift while also calling for vital change in the patterns of gender discrimination and other injustices—notably racism, discrimination and discriminations based on sex—that continue to be voiced in contemporary gaming and streaming. Being a citizen in live-video politics is fundamentally tied to what a wider Twitch community is willing to accept or erase from view. Recall in Chapter 2 how Sumail, a Pakistani immigrant gamer of colour, was so quickly racialized by gamers in chat despite being lauded as the youngest Esports gaming champion ever to win the Internationals Dota 2 tournament, his likeness compared in emoji-form to the terrorists who attacked the World Trade Centre on 9/11. Despite his significant corporate backing and his masses of adoring fans, Sumail was not permitted to serve as an unalloyed poster-boy for the gaming industry, nor was he allowed to stand in as the model figure of a lucrative professionalized gamer. Though a wide majority of gamers in chat refused to accept any unfair treatment of Sumail, a significant few refused to look beyond his immigrant past, choosing instead to imbue upon him racial characteristics of threatening difference.

It is worth noting that in her more recent work, Sherry Turkle, former champion of "life on the screen", raises troubling questions that are markedly less optimistic in tone than in her initial writing. She questions what our responsibility is towards ourselves and towards others in a world where we are now co-constructing "second selves" in machine worlds; the answer, somewhat a continuation of Putnam in *Bowling Alone* (2001), is that if we are concerned about facing a "democratic deficit" in contemporary times, it is because of the isolation caused by our new technologies, which promise so much but ultimately lead us to favour "robotic moments" over our "human purpose".[15] In Europe, despair over a digital generation has researchers, policymakers, and leaders longing for a bygone era of political activism, and lives more grounded in the "real". Geert Lovink writes in *Networks Without a Cause: Critique of Social Media* of the weak ties that form online:

> These days "the social" is a feature. It is no longer a problem (as in the nineteenth and twentieth centuries when the Social Problem predominated) or a sector in society provided for deviant, sick, and elderly people. Until recently, employing an amoral definition of the social was unthinkable ... Now the beast has been tamed ... The social lost its mysterious potential energy to burst suddenly onto the street and take power ... the trend is clear: the networks without cause are time eaters, and we're only being sucked deeper into the social cave without knowing what to look for.[16]

While this appears bleak for a digital age, we should ask whether young people truly are no longer learning to participate in civic and political life and if there could still be hope for the future of sociality and democracy in a digital age.[17]

The reality is that networks on Twitch do exhibit distinct activisms—gamers do in fact join political causes—only these may not always be aligned with the politics of mainstream studies or palatable to political pundits and organizations without video game affiliations. Add to this a resistance on behalf of scholars to pursue a force of "politics" that is not strictly engaged with global affairs, civil society, and/or the immediate concerns of the nation-state, and we have gamers set up to fail before even a full investigation into what being a citizen means to live-video politics. What is necessary is a reconfiguration of the notion of civic and

130 Conclusion

political life, a realignment of our goals for the future of a democracy in a digital age. To be clear, in this endeavour, gamers have not yet been entirely successful. The many struggles apparent on Twitch put the entire enterprise of live-video politics—one that is ultimately seeking to elevate all gamers to a level of respectability that might someday overcome a dominant discourse of disaffection—on tenuous ground. It is the community as a whole that troubles the politics of being citizens for gamers, and that community as a whole on Twitch remains fractured in vital places. As such, live streams both enable and constrain identities and practices in a digital age, and while this is indeed important to framing gamers beyond a logic of magic circles in virtual worlds, it also implies a complex of both being and becoming that is yet to fully resolve for gamer subjects.

As Engin Isin and Evelyn Ruppert articulate best in *Being Digital Citizens* (2015):

> Let us now describe cyberspace as a space of **transactions and interactions between and among bodies acting through the Internet** … If indeed cyberspace is first a relational space, these relations are between and among bodies through the Internet. These bodies can be collective (institutions, organizations, corporations, collectives, groups), cybernetic, or social. Finally, these acting **bodies are neither subservient nor sovereign subjects** (my emphasis added).[18]

This description highlights the very important reminder that the internet does not substitute or replace bodies in physical space. The internet is not simply a network of networks but rather a network of people. It is not necessarily an agonistic separate body or an independent entity; rather, it is a space of relations between situated bodies. As such, live-video politics is not necessarily a way out of past and ongoing social injustices since virtual encounters on stream increasingly bring dominant and subordinate subjects into contact with each other. A live-video politics of being citizens involves new pronouncements as well as familiar old ones, together serving as reminders that it is time to change our expectations and our performances towards others; our bodies are neither subservient nor sovereign.

Being a citizen involves finding new and complex registers to interpret social interactions online. Isin and Ruppert go further in their own work *on being digital citizens* to claim that "cyberspace, then, is a complex space of "becoming citizens", and it is through digital acts that we uncover an emerging politics in a digital age.[19] Their contribution is to illustrate an emerging digital citizen who articulates "I, we, they have a right to" online and who also performs rights claims through a variety of "things" over the internet. For example, digital citizens engage with "participating", "connecting", and "sharing", and also "witnessing", "hacking", or "commoning"; these may take up more traditional forms of human and political rights, as for example in activist campaigns and NGO projects, but they might also engage in struggles over a new politics of information use, for example rights of expression, digital access, and privacy online. Digital citizens become refashioned, reconfigured, and re-signified in and through cyberspace.

Who is a digital citizen?, or more specifically, who is the subject of digital rights? These are, of course, urgent and political questions that need addressing, especially since subjects online are usually (with few exceptions) at once actual citizens with ties to communities, nations, and regions that have material needs, conflicts, and aspirations. These questions will all be important problems for gamers as citizens and inheritors of the incumbent democracy to answer. However, a live-video politics of being citizens evolves firstly out of virtual worlds and video games, which present accelerations and amplifications of a unique kind. Gamers as citizens first build agency and community; they fight to maintain control over the conditions of their labor; and finally, they must now address the problems of identity, inclusivity, and the radical potential transformations of themselves on streams.

We may rightly ask at this critical juncture: what will it take for the figure that we call Gamer Citizen to emerge? Such a figure, as we recall, is (1) not a learner but rather an expert; (2) not primarily disaffected but instead highly engaged and capable of sophisticated action as well as strong leadership; and (3) possessing a mastery and skill over the building of communities both online and offline.

I had many encounters during my time spent in the field, only a tiny fraction of which I have been able to share in these writings, but it is important to recall that my core inquiry, to ask "How are gamers political?", was not only designed to assemble a collection of narratives but to seek out new knowledge of citizens and to investigate the characteristics, forms, and directions of politics in a digital age. This was not to imply that online communities must necessarily be held to account strictly in terms of a contrast between what is "real" and what is virtual, but rather to operate on the premise that gamers create, inhabit, and inherit a political world that includes gaming, and that it is an important task to reveal what this politics entails for the future. What is any digital citizen's responsibility to the world offline? What is a gamer's responsibility? These will ultimately be the guiding questions of much future work.

132 Conclusion

QUESTIONS

1. What are the dimensions of a live video politics described in this chapter? Would you add any new characteristics?
2. Can you think of any recent examples of a live video politics?
3. Where is live video politics heading next? How might we change our approach to the study of Gamer Citizens in the future?

Notes

1 The endurance rating of most gaming mice exceeds 5 million clicks. The most recent successor to my mouse, the Logitech G502, is rated to 20 million clicks before failure.
2 GLHF—"Good luck, have fun".
3 World Health Organization (2018) ICD-11 Accessed 8/31/2018 URL: http://www.who.int/health-topics/international-classification-of-diseases.
4 Chen. A. (2018). "Ice Poseidon's Lucrative, Stressful Life as a Live Streamer" in The New Yorker, Annals of Technology. URL: https://www.newyorker.com/magazine/2018/07/09/ice-poseidons-lucrative-stressful-life-as-a-live-streamer.
5 Kücklich, j. (2014). "Precarious Playbour: Modders and the Digital Games Industry" in DOAJ Fibreculture Journal (Jan 2005) No.5 URL: https://doaj.org/article/8c55373d52334369b1708c1f0ac07fee; McGuigan, J. (2014) "The Neoliberal Self", Culture Unbound, 6(1), pp. 223–240.
6 Strub, C. (2020). "$83M+ Raised And Counting In 2020: Are Twitch Streamers The New Philanthropists?" in Forbes. URL: https://www.forbes.com/sites/chrisstrub/2020/12/18/83m-raised-and-counting-in-2020-are-twitch-streamers-the-new-philanthropists/?sh=65d640202e52.
7 Geyser, W. (2023). "How Much do Twitch Streamers Make? [+Twitch Media Value Money Calculator]" in Influencer Marketing Hub. URL: https://influencermarketinghub.com/twitch-money-calculator/.
8 Cohen, S. (1984). ZAP! the rise and fall of Atari. New York: McGraw-Hill; and Sheff, D. (1993). Game over: How Nintendo zapped an American industry, captured your dollars, and enslaved your children. New York: Random House.
9 McGuigan, J. (2014) "The Neoliberal Self", Culture Unbound, 6(1), p. 232.
10 Chess, S. (2017). *Ready Player Two Women Gamers and Designed Identity*. University of Minnesota Press Minneapolis London.
11 Code, L., & Oxford University Press. (2006). Ecological thinking: The politics of epistemic location. Oxford: Oxford University Press.
12 Phillips, A. (2020). *Gamer Trouble: Feminist Confrontations in Digital Culture*. New York University Press. New York
13 Patterson. B. C. (2020). *Open World Empire: Race, Erotics and The Global Rise of Video Games*. New York University Press. New York. p. 7.
14 Patterson. B. C. (2020). *Open World Empire: Race, Erotics and The Global Rise of Video Games*. New York University Press. New York.

Conclusion **133**

15 Turkle, S. (2011). Alone Together: Why We Expect More from Technology and Less from Each Other. Basic Books: New York; and Putnam, Robert D. (2001) Bowling Alone. Simon & Schuster Paperbacks: New York.
16 Lovink, Geert (2011). Networks Without a Cause: A Critique of Social Media. Polity Press: Cambridge; p. 6.
17 See: Bennett, W L (2008). Civic Life Online: Learning How Digital Media Can Engage Youth. Cambridge, Mass: MIT Press; Metzger, Miriam J, and Andrew J. Flanagin (2008). Digital Media, Youth, and Credibility. Cambridge, Mass: MIT Press; and McPherson, Tara (2008). Digital Youth, Innovation, and the Unexpected. Cambridge, Mass: MIT Press.
18 Isin, Engin. & Evelyn Ruppert (2015) Being Digital Citizens. Rowman & Littlefield Publishing Group; p. 14.
19 Ibid.

INDEX

Note: Page numbers in *italics* refer to figures.

abnormality 19
actualized citizen 31
affect *vs.* effect 47
Alexandria Ocasio-Cortez (AOC) 3–4
Among Us 15
Anele emoji 59, *60*
Anglo-American culture 27
anti-social video games 14
anxiety 1, 32, 34
Appelman, Robert L. 30
artificial intelligence 1–2
ATARI *see* Nintendo Entertainment
avatars 64–65, 69, *69*, 83, 84n2, 98
Azoulay, Ariella 52

Banaji, Shakuntala 27
Barab, S. 30
behavioural psychology 19
Being Digital Citizens (Isin and Ruppert) 4, 130–131
Bennet, W. Lance 28
Bers, Marina Umaschi 30
BibleThump 56, 58, 61
The Binding of Isaac 56
Black Lives Matter 28
broadcasting 17; community 15; *see also* streamingBuckingham, David 27

Caillois, R. 33
catharsis theory 35
Cesar, Pablo 6
charity gaming 17
charity streams 107–113
circuit of culture 45, 48, *48*; identity 56; nodes of 56; regulation 56; representation 56
civic activity 16, 28; education 28–32; engagement 27; play 31; websites 27
The Civil Contract of Photography 52
civil contracts 52–53
Civilization and *Sim City* (Squire and Barab) 30
Cognitive Psychology of Mass Communication (Harris and Sanborn) 19
cognitive thinking 1
Cohen, Scott 86
Comcast Cable Communications 113
communication 6
community 4–5
computer-mediated communication (CMC) 70, 72
conduct, regulation of 20
consumer: media industry 35; society 7
cool-capitalism 125
corporate infiltrations 87–96

Index **135**

Crack, Angela 9
Crawford, Garry 21
Critiques of everyday life (Gardiner) 7
currencies, video games 22
cyber-inhabitants 71
cyberspace 4, 71

Danesi, Marcel 47
DansGame 45–46, *46*, 59, 61
DC *see* dutiful citizenship
DDD *see* dominant discourse of disaffection
defiance of disaffection 15
DeGaetano, Gloria 19
Democracy 30
Democracy 2 30
digital age 7–8
digital assistants 11n1
digital citizens 4
Digital Dilemmas: Power, Resistance, and the Internet (Franklin) 10
discourse 20
dominant discourse of disaffection (DDD) 18–21
Don't Lurk on Democracy! campaign 15, *16*
doom scrolling 1
Dota 2 45, 118
dungeons 76–78
dutiful citizenship (DC) 28–29, 31

electronic amusements 22–23, 35
electronic-sport (E-Sport) 6
emojis: BibleThump 61; as civic duty 60–62; code 47–52; Dansgame 61; interventions 4; ResidentSleeper 61
enactments of citizenship 4
entrepreneurship 88
Esports gaming community 17

Falcao, T. 33
fame diagram 74
floating signifiers 48, 56
frames 10, 73, 75
Franklin, Marianne 9–10
fundraising 17

Gakuen Hetalia 65
Gal Gun 25
game: commentary 111; design 22; developers 50; plan 88; play online 5; publisher 77; studios 50; world 74

Game Over: How Nintendo Zapped an American Industry, Captured Your Dollars, and Enslaved Your Children (Sheff) 86
gamer citizens 4, 7, 15, 18, 35–36, 44–46, 53, 60; civil contracts 52–53; community activity 66; emoji code 47–52; emojis as civic duty 60–62; everyday life of 67; mentors, role-models, and imperial tracks 53–56; opening the circuit 56–60; social activities 65–66; *see also* gamers
gamer politics 14–18; civics education 28–32; disaffection and engagement 21–26; dominant discourse of disaffection (DDD) 18–21; internet and democracy 26–28; learner citizens 28–32; magic circles 18, 32–35; young citizens 26–28
gamers 3–4, 82–83; civic responsibility in 15; disaffection 18–21; on livestreams 2–3; *see also* gamer citizens
Games Developer Conference (GDC) 30
Games Done Quick streams (GDQs) 109–114, *110*; charity streams 109, 112
gaming: addiction 121; culture 126; disorder 121; economies 49; feats 113; for good 17; habits 82; social and cultural significance of 18
Gardiner, Michael E. 7
gaymers 17
GDC *see* Games Developer Conference
GDQs *see* Games Done Quick streams
Geerts, David 6
give away platform 89–90
Glas, Rene 73
Goffman, E. 73–74
Gosling, Victoria K. 21
Grand Theft Auto 25
graphical fidelity 68
Grossman, Dave 18–19
guardian player character 69
Guild Wars 2 67–81; artwork and graphics design 69; criticism 78–81; dungeons 76–78; modes 76; PvP 68; sPvP 67–69, 74

habit, damaging 18–19
Hall, Stuart 19, 48
hard work 91–96
Harris, Richard Jackson 19

136 Index

Hassan, Syed Sumail 44
Hearthstone 17
hegemonic bargain 61
Heller, Agnes 7
Hernandez, Patricia 16
High-Speed Society 53
homo-ludens 33
hosting 4
human activity systems 10
Huzinga, J. 33

identities, construction of 20
in-game gold 22
instagraming 1
intellectual thinking 35
international Statistical Classification
     of Diseases (ICD-11) 120–122
internet 2; bandwidth 5;
     gaming disorder 120; internet
     communication technologies (ICT) 9
Isin, Engin 4, 130

Kaytoue, M. 6
Kücklich, Julian 124

LANscapes 10
learner citizens 18, 28–32
Lefebvre, Henri 7
*Let the Games Begin: Civic Playing on
     High-Tech Consoles* (Bers) 30
LGBTQ+ communities 17
lifeworlds 10
Light, Ben 21
linguists 47–48
live chat: functionality 88; moderating 4
Liveegg 92, 125–126
live video: platform 5; politics 8,
     119–120, 126; streams 4–5, 64
Lovink, Geert 2, 129
ludic divide: charity streams 107–113;
     corporate infiltrations 87–96;
     viewership as co-labour 96–107
ludologists 33, 115n4

machine–human social relations 23
magic circles 10, 18, 32–35, 64, 73
McGonigal, Jane 22
McGuigan, Jim 124–125
media centric 9
media violence 19
Medicins Sans Frontier 112
mental health disorders 19

mentors, role-models, and imperial
     tracks 53–56
metaverse 1
mouse 117
multiplayer games 67–70

narratologist 115n4
Negroponte, Nicholas 73
neoliberalism 124
neo-liberal self 124–126
*Networks Without a Cause: Critique
     of Social Media* 129
Next 36 88–89
Nintendo 86
Nintendo 64 game console 93, 103
Nintendo Entertainment 86, 125
nostalgia 64–65

object games 34
online games: *Among Us* 15; *Grand
     Theft Auto* 25; *Rapeplay* 25;
     Saints Row 25; *Second Life* 24–25;
     Superpower 31; *Wordslinger* 24–25;
     see also video games
*Online Gaming in Context: The Social
     and Cultural Significance of Online
     Gaming* (Crawford, Light, and
     Gosling) 21
online sociality 118
On the Campaign Trail 30
opening the circuit 56–60; floating
     signifiers 56

participatory culture 108–113
Patterson, Christoper B. 127
Philips, Amanda 127
platform 10
*Play Between Worlds: Exploring
     Online Game Culture* (Taylor) 82
political campaigns 28
political decision-making process 30
populism 27
Positech Games 30
positionality 52
power 20
production 48
punWaifu emoji 100
PvP 68

random number generation (rng) 102,
     116n11
Rank, Allison 28

Rapeplay 25
reification 122
ResidentSleeper 59, 61
Rheingold, Howard 70–73
Ribeiro, Jose Carlos 33
Ruppert, Evelyn 4, 130

Saints Row 25
Salen, K. 33
same-sex couples 17
Sanborn, Fred W. 19
sanctioned play paradigm 23
Scuf Gaming 118
Second Life 24–25
self-actualized citizens (AC) 28–29
self-reflexivity 58
serious games 30
sexual violence 24
Sheff, David 86
Shira Chess 127
sign-vehicles 48
single-issue organizations
    networks 28
Smith, Dorothy E. 7
social and cultural significance of
    gaming 17
social capital 25
social frame theory 73
social learning theory 35
social TV 6, 9
socio-material life 7
specter of entrepreneurship 87
speculative hyperbole 34
speedrunners 87, 93, 126
sPvP (structured Player *versus* Player)
    67; world map 68
Squire, K. 30
state centric media 10
Steelseries Rival 600 117–118
Stop Teaching Our Kids to Kill
    (Grossman and DeGaetano) 18
stream donating 4
streamers 90
streaming 4–5, 9; events 17, 71, 72;
    world 74; *see also* live video
subjectivities, construction of 20
subscribing 4
Sumail Hassan, Syed (video game
    player) 44–46, 49, 49–60, 118
Super Mario 64 65, 87, 93, 98, 101,
    103, 113; speedrunner 102, 104
Superpower 31

Taylor, T. L. 82
TeamSpeak 69
techno centric media 10
techno-sociality 25
Thornham, Helen 23
tik toking 1
top-of-the-line device 117
tournament organizers 50
Triple Trouble 109
Turkle, Sherry 73
Twitch 6, 15, 44–45, 53, 59, 65, 123;
    Emojis 46; marketing tagline 54
TwitchCon 120

valorize Esports 50
Valve Corporation 49–50, 53–55, 59
video games 22; *The Binding of
    Isaac* 56; *On the Campaign Trail*
    30; currencies 22; defined 32;
    Democracy 30; *Democracy 2*
    30; *Dota 2* 45; engagement and
    social contact 21; *Gal Gun* 25;
    Guild Wars 2 67–70; social and
    cultural significance 23; space 10;
    spectatorship 5; *Super Mario 64*
    65, 87; theory 64; virtual spaces,
    characteristics, and relationships
    64–66; *World of Warcraft* 22;
    see also online games
video streaming service 5
viewership as co-labour 96–107
violent entertainment 19
violent video games 14, 18
virtual battlefield 67
virtual communities 70–73, 82–83
virtual world 33
voice communication 69
voice-over-the-internet protocol
    (VOIP) software 69

Wajcman, Judy 34
*Watch Me Playing, I am a
    Professional: a First Study on Video
    Game Live Streaming* (Kaytoue) 6
web-based development business 88
web designers 87
Wells, Chris 28
Williams, Raymond 7
Witkowski, E. 7
Women's Marches 28
WonderCon 120
Wordslinger 24–25

138 Index

World of Warcraft 22
World Pride 28

Xfinity 118

Yang, Charlie 45
YouTube 5

zap 125
Zap: The Rise and Fall of ATARI (Cohen) 86
Zimmerman, E. 33

Printed in the United States
by Baker & Taylor Publisher Services